Dealing with Manipulative People in Your Life

Unlock the Secrets to Recognizing and Stopping
Emotional Abuse, Gaslighting, and
Psychological Manipulation

Liz Ben

Table of Contents

Introduction

Manipulation and abuse within relationships are often like an invisible poison, gradually corroding trust, self-esteem, and emotional well-being. They can occur in various forms and intensities, making it difficult for victims to recognize and confront them. To effectively combat these toxic dynamics, it is essential to understand what manipulation and abuse entail, how they manifest, and why awareness and education are crucial in addressing these issues.

Manipulation in relationships involves exerting influence over someone through deceptive, exploitative, or coercive means to achieve one's own ends. Unlike healthy influence, which respects the autonomy and integrity of others, manipulation seeks to control and diminish. It often involves subtle tactics that can be hard to pinpoint, such as guilt-tripping, playing the victim, or using charm to disarm and control.

Abuse, on the other hand, encompasses a broader spectrum of behaviors that are designed to dominate, belittle, and harm another person. This can be physical, but more often, it manifests as emotional and psychological abuse. Emotional abuse aims to erode the victim's sense of self-worth and independence through constant criticism, humiliation, and isolation. Psychological abuse, similarly, manipulates the victim's mind and emotions to create confusion, fear, and dependency.

Overview of Emotional Abuse, Gaslighting, and Psychological Manipulation

Emotional abuse is a systematic pattern of behavior that undermines a person's self-esteem and emotional stability. It can include verbal assaults, dominance, control, isolation, ridicule, and other tactics aimed at weakening the victim's mental and emotional health. Victims often find themselves questioning their reality, feeling worthless, and becoming increasingly dependent on the abuser for validation and approval.

Gaslighting is a particularly insidious form of psychological manipulation. It involves making the victim doubt their own memories, perceptions, and sanity. The term originates from the 1944 film "Gaslight," where a husband manipulates his wife into believing she is losing her mind. Modern gaslighting can take many forms, from outright denial of facts to subtle undermining of the victim's confidence in their judgment. Over time, this tactic can erode a person's reality, making them entirely reliant on the manipulator's version of events.

Psychological manipulation encompasses various strategies aimed at controlling and exploiting others. This can include emotional blackmail, where the manipulator uses fear, obligation, and guilt to control the victim's actions. It can also involve more sophisticated tactics, such as playing on the victim's deepest fears and desires, or leveraging social dynamics and personal insecurities to bend the victim's will. The ultimate goal is always control and domination, achieved through mental and emotional coercion.

Importance of Awareness and Education on These Topics

Understanding and recognizing manipulation and abuse are the first steps toward breaking free from their grasp. Awareness allows individuals to identify unhealthy patterns in their relationships and take proactive steps to protect themselves. It also empowers bystanders and loved ones to support victims more effectively, creating a network of awareness and support that can make a significant difference.

Education on these topics is crucial not only for victims but also for society at large. It fosters a culture of respect, empathy, and vigilance against abusive behaviors. By educating people about the signs and tactics of manipulation and abuse, we can create a more informed and resilient community. This knowledge equips individuals with the tools to assert their boundaries, recognize red flags, and seek help when needed.

Moreover, education can challenge and change societal norms that perpetuate abuse and manipulation. It can help dismantle myths and misconceptions that blame victims or normalize abusive behaviors. By fostering an environment where manipulation and abuse are understood and condemned, we contribute to a culture that prioritizes healthy, respectful, and empowering relationships.

Recognizing and Addressing Manipulation and Abuse

Recognizing manipulation and abuse requires keen awareness and a willingness to confront uncomfortable truths. Many victims live in a state of denial or minimization, believing that the abuse is their fault or that it isn't as bad as it seems. This is often reinforced by the manipulator, who may use gaslighting or other tactics to maintain control. However, recognizing the signs of abuse is the first step toward liberation.

Common signs of manipulation and abuse include feeling constantly criticized or belittled, experiencing extreme mood swings from the manipulator, feeling isolated from friends and family, and doubting one's own judgment and reality. Victims may also feel a sense of walking on eggshells, constantly trying to avoid triggering the manipulator's anger or displeasure.

Addressing these issues involves several steps. First, it is important to acknowledge the reality of the situation. This may involve talking to trusted friends or family members, seeking professional help from a therapist or counselor, or educating oneself through reliable resources. Support networks are vital in providing validation, guidance, and practical assistance.

Setting boundaries is another crucial step. This can be challenging, as manipulators often resist losing control and may escalate their tactics in response. However, establishing clear and firm boundaries is essential for protecting one's mental and emotional health. This might include limiting contact with the manipulator, refusing to engage in certain conversations, or seeking legal protection if necessary.

Finally, it is important to prioritize self-care and healing. Manipulation and abuse can leave deep emotional scars, and recovery is often a long and difficult process. Self-care involves nurturing one's physical, emotional, and psychological well-being. This can include therapy, support groups, engaging in hobbies and activities that bring joy and fulfillment, and building a strong, supportive network of friends and loved ones.

Promoting Healthy Relationships and Resilience
Promoting healthy relationships involves cultivating respect, empathy, and open communication. It requires recognizing and valuing each person's autonomy and boundaries. Healthy relationships are built on mutual trust, support, and equality, where both parties feel safe, respected, and valued.

Resilience in the face of manipulation and abuse is about developing the inner strength and resources to withstand and overcome adversity. This involves building self-esteem, fostering self-awareness, and cultivating a sense of empowerment and agency. Resilience also means learning to recognize and resist manipulation tactics, and having the courage to seek help and make difficult decisions when necessary.

The Role of Society in Addressing Manipulation and Abuse
Society plays a crucial role in addressing manipulation and abuse. This involves creating awareness, providing education, and offering support and resources for victims. It also means challenging and changing cultural norms that perpetuate abusive behaviors and victim-blaming.

Educational programs in schools, workplaces, and communities can raise awareness and provide people with the knowledge and skills to recognize and address manipulation and abuse. Media campaigns and public service announcements can also play a significant role in spreading awareness and changing societal attitudes.

Support services such as hotlines, shelters, counseling, and legal assistance are vital in providing practical help for victims. These services need to be accessible, well-funded, and staffed by trained professionals who can offer empathetic and informed support.

Legal frameworks and policies are also important in providing protection for victims and holding abusers accountable. This involves not only criminalizing abusive behaviors but also ensuring that victims have access to justice and support services.

Understanding manipulation and abuse is a critical step towards breaking free from their toxic grip. By recognizing the signs, understanding the tactics, and equipping oneself with knowledge and resources, individuals can protect themselves and foster healthy, respectful relationships. Awareness and education are powerful tools in this journey, enabling people to identify, confront, and overcome manipulation and abuse. As a society, we must work together to promote a culture of respect, empathy, and empowerment, ensuring that everyone has the opportunity to live free from manipulation and abuse.

Chapter 1

The Psychology Behind Manipulation

Manipulation is a deeply complex and troubling aspect of human interaction, often rooted in the psychological underpinnings of both the manipulator and the victim. To effectively address and counteract manipulation, it is essential to understand the motivations and goals of manipulators, as well as the psychological theories and frameworks that explain these behaviors. It explores these elements in detail, shedding light on why manipulation occurs and how it can be recognized and addressed.

Understanding the Motivations and Goals of Manipulators

At its core, manipulation is about control. Manipulators seek to control the thoughts, feelings, and actions of others to fulfill their own needs and desires. These needs can vary widely but often include power, attention, validation, and security. By manipulating others, individuals can gain a sense of superiority, self-worth, or safety that they might not be able to achieve through honest and direct means.

One primary motivation for manipulation is the desire for power. Manipulators often feel a deep need to dominate others, to be in control of their environment and the people within it. This need for power can stem from a variety of sources, including past trauma, insecurity, or an inherent personality trait. In many cases, manipulators may have experienced situations in their own lives where they felt powerless or victimized, leading them to adopt manipulative behaviors as a way to regain control.

Attention and validation are other significant motivators for manipulators. Many individuals who engage in manipulative behaviors crave the attention and approval of others. They may use manipulation to draw people closer, to be the center of attention, or to feel important and valued. This can be particularly evident in narcissistic individuals, who often have an inflated sense of self-importance and a deep need for admiration and affirmation.

Security is another driving force behind manipulation. Some manipulators feel an intense fear of abandonment or rejection and use manipulation to ensure that others stay close to them. By controlling the emotions and actions of those around them, they can create a sense of stability and predictability in their relationships. This need for security can be rooted in early childhood experiences or past relationships where they felt neglected or abandoned.

Ultimately, the goals of manipulators are often self-serving and centered on maintaining their sense of control, power, and self-worth. They may not always be consciously aware of their motivations, but their behaviors are consistently aimed at achieving these underlying goals. By understanding these motivations, individuals can better recognize and address manipulative behaviors in their own lives.

Psychological Theories and Frameworks Related to Manipulation

Several psychological theories and frameworks help to explain the phenomenon of manipulation and the behaviors of those who engage in it. These theories provide valuable insights into the underlying mechanisms that drive manipulative actions and offer a foundation for developing strategies to counteract them.

One relevant framework is the concept of the "dark triad" of personality traits, which includes narcissism, Machiavellianism, and psychopathy. Individuals who exhibit these traits are more likely to engage in manipulative behaviors. Narcissists, with their grandiose sense of self-importance and need for admiration, often use manipulation to maintain their inflated self-image and to keep others in a state of dependence. Machiavellianism, characterized by a strategic and manipulative approach to social interactions, involves the calculated use of deceit and exploitation to achieve personal goals. Psychopathy, marked by a lack of empathy and remorse, can lead to manipulative behaviors that are cold, calculated, and devoid of genuine emotional connection.

Attachment theory also offers valuable insights into manipulation. According to this theory, early experiences with caregivers shape an individual's attachment style, which in turn influences their relationships throughout life. Those with insecure attachment styles, such as anxious or avoidant attachment, may be more prone to engaging in manipulative behaviors as a way to manage their fears of rejection and abandonment. Anxiously attached individuals might use manipulation to keep others close and to avoid being left alone, while avoidantly attached individuals might manipulate to maintain emotional distance and protect themselves from vulnerability.

Cognitive-behavioral theories suggest that manipulation can be learned through observation and reinforcement. Individuals may develop manipulative behaviors by observing others who use these tactics successfully or by experiencing positive outcomes when they engage in manipulation themselves. Over time, these behaviors become reinforced and ingrained, making them a habitual way of interacting with others. This perspective highlights the importance of addressing and changing these learned behaviors through awareness and intervention.

The concept of emotional intelligence also plays a significant role in understanding manipulation. Emotional intelligence involves the ability to recognize, understand, and manage one's own emotions, as well as the emotions of others. Manipulators often have a high degree of emotional intelligence in the sense that they can accurately perceive and exploit the emotions of their victims. However, their use of emotional intelligence is skewed toward manipulation rather than genuine empathy and connection. By improving their own emotional intelligence, individuals can become more adept at recognizing manipulative tactics and responding in ways that protect their emotional well-being.

Recognizing and Counteracting Manipulative Behaviors

Recognizing manipulative behaviors is a critical step in protecting oneself from their harmful effects. Manipulative tactics can take many forms, from subtle emotional manipulation to more overt forms of control and coercion. Some common signs of manipulation include constant criticism, guilt-tripping, playing the victim, gaslighting, and creating a sense of dependency or obligation.

One effective strategy for recognizing manipulation is to pay attention to how interactions with a particular person make you feel. If you frequently feel confused, anxious, guilty, or diminished after interacting with someone, it may be a sign that they are using manipulative tactics. Trusting your instincts and feelings can be a powerful tool in identifying and addressing manipulation.

Setting clear and firm boundaries is another essential strategy for counteracting manipulation. Boundaries are the limits you set regarding what you will and will not tolerate in your relationships. By establishing and maintaining these boundaries, you can protect yourself from being controlled or exploited by others. This may involve communicating your boundaries explicitly, enforcing consequences for boundary violations, and being willing to distance yourself from individuals who repeatedly disrespect your boundaries.

Developing self-awareness and self-esteem is also crucial in counteracting manipulation. Manipulators often prey on individuals who have low self-esteem or who are unaware of their own needs and vulnerabilities. By building a strong sense of self-worth and becoming more attuned to your own emotions and needs, you can reduce your susceptibility to manipulation. This may involve engaging in self-reflection, seeking therapy or counseling, and surrounding yourself with supportive and affirming relationships.

Empathy and Understanding in the Face of Manipulation

While it is essential to protect oneself from manipulation, it is also important to approach the issue with empathy and understanding. Manipulative behaviors often stem from deep-seated fears, insecurities, and unmet needs. By recognizing the underlying motivations behind these behaviors, individuals can respond with compassion rather than anger or resentment.

This does not mean tolerating or excusing manipulative behaviors, but rather approaching the situation with a balanced perspective. Understanding that manipulators are often driven by their own pain and fear can help individuals respond in ways that are both protective and compassionate. This might involve setting firm boundaries while also offering support and understanding when appropriate.

The Role of Support Networks and Professional Help

Dealing with manipulation and abuse can be incredibly challenging, and having a strong support network is vital. Friends, family, and support groups can provide emotional support, validation, and practical advice. They can help individuals recognize manipulative behaviors, reinforce boundaries, and offer encouragement and assistance in difficult situations.

Professional help, such as therapy or counseling, can also be invaluable in addressing the psychological impact of manipulation and abuse. Therapists can help individuals develop coping strategies, build self-esteem, and work through the emotional trauma associated with manipulation. They can also provide guidance on setting and maintaining boundaries, navigating difficult relationships, and fostering healthier patterns of interaction.

Building Resilience and Empowerment

Ultimately, the goal of understanding manipulation and its psychological underpinnings is to build resilience and empowerment. By recognizing the tactics and motivations of manipulators, individuals can develop the strength and confidence to protect themselves and foster healthier relationships.

Resilience involves the ability to withstand and recover from adversity. It requires developing a strong sense of self-worth, emotional intelligence, and the skills to navigate complex social interactions. Empowerment involves taking control of one's own life, making informed decisions, and asserting one's needs and boundaries.

Building resilience and empowerment is a continuous process that involves self-reflection, learning, and growth. It requires a commitment to self-care, self-awareness, and the ongoing development of healthy relationship skills. By embracing this journey, individuals can create a life that is free from manipulation and abuse, characterized by respect, empathy, and genuine connection.

Understanding the psychology behind manipulation is a crucial step in addressing and counteracting its harmful effects. By exploring the motivations and goals of manipulators, as well as the psychological theories and frameworks that explain these behaviors, individuals can gain valuable insights into why manipulation occurs and how it can be recognized and addressed. Recognizing manipulative behaviors, setting boundaries, developing self-awareness and self-esteem, and seeking support are all essential strategies in this process. Ultimately, the goal is to build resilience and empowerment, fostering healthier and more respectful relationships. By embracing this journey, individuals can create a life characterized by genuine connection, respect, and emotional well-being.

Chapter 2

How Manipulators Exploit Vulnerabilities

Manipulation is a pervasive and insidious force that can infiltrate various aspects of our lives, from personal relationships to professional environments. Understanding how manipulators exploit vulnerabilities is crucial for protecting oneself and fostering healthier interactions. The common tactics used by manipulators are revealed, also it shows how to recognize subtle signs of manipulation, and provide case studies and examples to illustrate these behaviors in different contexts.

Identifying Manipulation Tactics

Manipulators employ a wide range of tactics to control, influence, and exploit others. These tactics are often subtle and insidious, making them difficult to recognize. However, by becoming familiar with these strategies, individuals can better identify and defend against manipulation.

Gaslighting

Gaslighting is a form of psychological manipulation where the manipulator makes the victim doubt their own perceptions, memories, and sanity. This tactic involves the repeated denial of facts, distortion of reality, and deliberate misinformation. Over time, the victim may begin to question their own reality, leading to confusion, anxiety, and a diminished sense of self-worth.

Guilt-Tripping

Manipulators often use guilt as a tool to control others. By making the victim feel guilty for their actions, choices, or even their feelings, the manipulator can elicit compliance and control. Phrases like "If you really loved me, you would..." or "After all I've done for you..." are common guilt-tripping tactics.

Playing the Victim

By portraying themselves as the victim, manipulators can evoke sympathy and manipulate others into fulfilling their needs. This tactic often involves exaggerating or fabricating personal struggles, hardships, or illnesses to gain attention, support, and control over others.

Love-Bombing

Love-bombing is a tactic where the manipulator showers the victim with excessive affection, attention, and compliments to create a sense of dependency and control. This tactic is often used in the initial stages of a relationship to quickly establish an emotional bond and gain the victim's trust and loyalty.

Triangulation

Triangulation involves manipulating relationships by bringing a third party into the dynamic. This tactic can be used to create jealousy, competition, and division among individuals, allowing the manipulator to maintain control and power. Triangulation can also involve pitting people against each other to deflect attention from the manipulator's actions.

Projection

Projection is a defense mechanism where the manipulator attributes their own negative traits, behaviors, or feelings to the victim. By projecting their flaws onto others, the manipulator can avoid taking responsibility for their actions and create confusion and self-doubt in the victim.

Isolation

Manipulators often seek to isolate their victims from friends, family, and support networks. By creating physical or emotional distance, the manipulator can increase the victim's dependency on them and reduce the likelihood of outside interference or support.

Recognizing Subtle Signs of Manipulation

Manipulation is not always overt or easily recognizable. Often, it manifests in subtle ways that can be easily overlooked or dismissed. Recognizing these subtle signs is essential for identifying and addressing manipulation before it escalates.

Inconsistent Behavior

Manipulators often exhibit inconsistent behavior, shifting between extremes of kindness and cruelty, affection and indifference, or support and criticism. These fluctuations can create confusion and keep the victim off balance, making it difficult to predict or respond to the manipulator's actions.

Disregard for Boundaries

Manipulators frequently disregard or violate personal boundaries, whether physical, emotional, or psychological. This can include invading personal space, pressuring for personal information, or ignoring requests for privacy and autonomy.

Excessive Charm

While charm itself is not inherently manipulative, excessive charm can be a red flag. Manipulators often use charm to gain trust and create a positive impression, only to later reveal their true intentions. This charm can be particularly disarming and make it difficult to recognize manipulative behavior.

Blame-Shifting

Manipulators are skilled at deflecting responsibility and blame onto others. When confronted with their actions, they may respond with defensiveness, denial, or accusations. This blame-shifting can create confusion and make it difficult for the victim to hold the manipulator accountable.

Emotional Outbursts

Frequent and unpredictable emotional outbursts can be a tactic to keep the victim on edge and maintain control. These outbursts may be used to intimidate, guilt-trip, or manipulate the victim into compliance.

Backhanded Compliments

Manipulators often use backhanded compliments or subtle put-downs to undermine the victim's self-esteem and confidence. These comments may be disguised as jokes or constructive criticism, making it difficult for the victim to recognize the manipulation.

Case Studies and Examples of Manipulation in Different Contexts

To illustrate the tactics and signs of manipulation, let's explore several case studies and examples from different contexts, including personal relationships, professional environments, and social interactions.

Personal Relationships

In personal relationships, manipulation can take many forms, from romantic partnerships to friendships and family dynamics. Consider the case of Sarah and Mark. Mark frequently uses gaslighting tactics to make Sarah doubt her own perceptions and memories. Whenever Sarah confronts Mark about his behavior, he denies it, accuses her of being overly sensitive, and suggests that she is imagining things. Over time, Sarah begins to question her own reality and feels increasingly anxious and isolated.

Another example is Lisa and her friend, Emily. Emily often plays the victim, exaggerating her personal struggles to gain Lisa's sympathy and support. Whenever Lisa tries to set boundaries or prioritize her own needs, Emily guilt-trips her by saying, "I thought you were my best friend. How can you be so selfish?" As a result, Lisa feels compelled to prioritize Emily's needs over her own, even when it is detrimental to her well-being.

Professional Environments

In the workplace, manipulation can manifest in various ways, from power dynamics to office politics. Consider the case of John and his colleague, Karen. Karen frequently uses triangulation to create competition and division among team members. She often shares gossip and confidential information with different colleagues, pitting them against each other and creating a tense and hostile work environment. By doing so, Karen maintains control and positions herself as a central figure in the office dynamic.

In another scenario, Michael's boss, David, uses love-bombing to manipulate him into working long hours and taking on additional responsibilities. David showers Michael with praise, recognition, and promises of promotion, creating a sense of loyalty and dependency. However, when Michael expresses concerns about his workload or requests time off, David becomes distant and critical, making Michael feel guilty and unappreciated.

Social Interactions

Manipulation can also occur in broader social interactions, including community groups, social circles, and online interactions. Consider the case of Rachel, who is part of a community organization. One of the group leaders, Tom, frequently uses projection to manipulate group dynamics. Whenever conflicts arise, Tom blames others for causing problems, projecting his own negative behaviors onto them. This creates confusion and division within the group, making it difficult to address the underlying issues.

In an online context, consider the case of Alex, who is part of an online gaming community. A fellow gamer, Sam, uses excessive charm and flattery to gain Alex's trust and access to his personal information. Once Sam has gained Alex's trust, he begins to pressure Alex into sharing more personal details and participating in activities that make Alex uncomfortable. When Alex expresses his concerns, Sam uses blame-shifting and emotional outbursts to manipulate him into compliance.

Empowerment and Strategies for Dealing with Manipulation

Recognizing manipulation is the first step toward addressing and countering it. Empowering oneself with knowledge, tools, and strategies is essential for maintaining healthy and strong relationships. Here are several strategies for dealing with manipulation:

Establish and Enforce Boundaries

Setting clear and firm boundaries is crucial for protecting oneself from manipulation. Communicate your limits and expectations clearly, and enforce consequences for boundary violations. This may involve distancing yourself from manipulative individuals or seeking support from trusted friends, family, or professionals.

Develop Emotional Intelligence

Improving emotional intelligence can help individuals recognize and respond to manipulative tactics more effectively. This involves becoming more aware of your own emotions, as well as the emotions of others, and developing skills for managing and expressing these emotions in healthy ways.

Seek Support

Having a strong support network is essential for dealing with manipulation. Friends, family, support groups, and professionals can provide emotional support, validation, and practical advice. They can help you recognize manipulative behaviors, reinforce boundaries, and offer encouragement and assistance in difficult situations.

Practice Self-Care

Taking care of your own emotional and physical well-being is crucial for building resilience against manipulation. Engage in activities that promote self-care, such as exercise, hobbies, meditation, and spending time with supportive and affirming people. Prioritize your own needs and well-being, and avoid sacrificing them for the sake of others.

Educate Yourself

Knowledge is a powerful tool for counteracting manipulation. Educate yourself about the tactics used by manipulators and the psychological mechanisms that drive these behaviors. By becoming more informed, you can better recognize and address manipulation in your own life.

Manipulation is a pervasive and harmful force that can infiltrate various aspects of our lives. By understanding the common tactics used by manipulators, recognizing subtle signs of manipulation, and exploring case studies and examples, individuals can become better equipped to identify and address these behaviors. Empowering oneself with knowledge, tools, and strategies is essential for maintaining healthy and strong relationships. By establishing boundaries, developing emotional intelligence, seeking support, practicing self-care, and educating oneself, individuals can build resilience and protect themselves from manipulation. Ultimately, the goal is to foster relationships characterized by respect, empathy, and genuine connection, free from the harmful effects of manipulation.

Chapter 3

Emotional Abuse: Recognizing and Addressing the Signs

Emotional abuse is a silent and insidious force that can leave deep, lasting scars on its victims. Unlike physical abuse, which manifests in visible wounds and bruises, emotional abuse often operates in the shadows, causing profound psychological and emotional damage. It aims to shed light on the various types of emotional abuse, the devastating impact it has on victims, and the steps individuals can take to recognize and address it.

Types of Emotional Abuse

Emotional abuse can take many forms, each uniquely damaging. Understanding these forms is the first step in recognizing and addressing emotional abuse.

Verbal Abuse

Verbal abuse includes shouting, name-calling, insults, and other forms of derogatory language. It is designed to demean, belittle, and undermine the victim's self-worth. For instance, a partner who constantly calls their significant other "stupid" or "worthless" is engaging in verbal abuse.

Gaslighting

Gaslighting is a form of psychological manipulation where the abuser makes the victim doubt their own perceptions, memories, and sanity. By persistently denying the victim's experiences and feelings, the abuser erodes their sense of reality. A common gaslighting tactic is for the abuser to insist that the victim is "overreacting" or "imagining things" when they express concerns.

Isolation

Isolation involves cutting the victim off from friends, family, and other support networks. By controlling who the victim interacts with and limiting their social contacts, the abuser increases their dependency and control. An abuser might insist on knowing the victim's whereabouts at all times and discourage or forbid them from seeing certain people.

Humiliation

Humiliation is used to degrade the victim and destroy their self-esteem. This can be done publicly or privately, through actions such as mocking, ridiculing, or embarrassing the victim. An abuser might make fun of the victim's appearance, intelligence, or abilities in front of others to make them feel inferior.

Control and Dominance

Abusers often exert control over various aspects of the victim's life, including their finances, activities, and decisions. This control is meant to dominate and restrict the victim's independence. For example, an abuser might control the household money, dictating how much the victim can spend and on what.

Emotional Blackmail

Emotional blackmail involves using fear, guilt, or obligation to manipulate the victim into compliance. The abuser may threaten to harm themselves or others if the victim does not comply with their demands. Statements like, "If you leave me, I'll hurt myself," are common examples of emotional blackmail.

Blaming and Shaming

Abusers often shift blame onto the victim for their own abusive behaviors. By making the victim feel responsible for the abuse, they perpetuate feelings of guilt and shame. An abuser might say, "If you hadn't made me so angry, I wouldn't have had to yell at you."

Impact of Emotional Abuse on Victims

The impact of emotional abuse is profound and far-reaching. It affects every aspect of a victim's life, from their mental health to their relationships and overall well-being.

Mental Health

Emotional abuse can lead to a range of mental health issues, including anxiety, depression, and post-traumatic stress disorder (PTSD). Victims often experience feelings of worthlessness, hopelessness, and chronic stress. The constant barrage of negativity and manipulation can erode their self-esteem and self-worth, leading to severe psychological distress.

Physical Health

The stress and anxiety caused by emotional abuse can manifest in physical health problems. Victims may experience headaches, digestive issues, chronic pain, and sleep disturbances. The body's prolonged response to stress can weaken the immune system, making them more susceptible to illness.

Relationships

Emotional abuse can damage the victim's ability to trust and form healthy relationships. They may become isolated, withdrawn, and fearful of intimacy. The abuser's tactics can cause the victim to question their own judgment and push away supportive friends and family members, leading to further isolation.

Self-Esteem and Identity

One of the most devastating impacts of emotional abuse is the destruction of the victim's self-esteem and sense of identity. Constant criticism, belittling, and manipulation can make the victim feel unworthy and unlovable. They may internalize the abuser's negative messages, leading to a distorted self-image and diminished self-confidence.

Life Opportunities

Emotional abuse can limit the victim's opportunities for personal and professional growth. The abuser's control and manipulation can prevent the victim from pursuing education, career advancement, and other life goals. The fear and self-doubt instilled by the abuser can also hinder the victim's ability to take risks and seize new opportunities.

Steps to Identify and Confront Emotional Abuse

Recognizing emotional abuse is the first step toward addressing it. The following steps can help individuals identify and confront emotional abuse in their lives.

Recognize the Signs

Awareness is key to recognizing emotional abuse. Pay attention to patterns of behavior that undermine your self-worth, isolate you from support networks, and make you doubt your reality. Trust your instincts and acknowledge your feelings. If something feels wrong, it likely is.

Document the Abuse

Keeping a record of abusive incidents can help validate your experiences and provide evidence if needed. Document instances of verbal abuse, gaslighting, isolation, and other forms of emotional abuse. Note the date, time, and context of each incident. This can also help you see patterns in the abuser's behavior.

Seek Support

Reaching out for support is crucial for dealing with emotional abuse. Talk to trusted friends, family members, or a mental health professional. Support groups and hotlines can also provide guidance and validation. Sharing your experiences with others can help you feel less isolated and more empowered.

Establish Boundaries

Setting and enforcing boundaries is essential for protecting yourself from further abuse. Clearly communicate your limits to the abuser and assertively enforce them. This may involve limiting contact, refusing to engage in certain conversations, or seeking physical separation.

Develop a Safety Plan

If you are in an abusive relationship, creating a safety plan can help protect you in case the situation escalates. This plan might include identifying a safe place to go, keeping important documents and emergency contacts accessible, and having a packed bag ready in case you need to leave quickly.

Educate Yourself

Learning about emotional abuse and manipulation can empower you to recognize and confront it. Read books, articles, and resources on the topic. Understanding the dynamics of abuse and the tactics used by abusers can help you see your situation more clearly and make informed decisions.

Practice Self-Care

Taking care of your mental and physical well-being is crucial when dealing with emotional abuse. Engage in activities that promote relaxation, happiness, and self-affirmation. This can include exercise, hobbies, meditation, and spending time with supportive and positive people.

Consider Professional Help

Therapy can be a valuable tool for dealing with the effects of emotional abuse. A mental health professional can help you process your experiences, build self-esteem, and develop coping strategies. Therapy can also provide a safe space to explore your feelings and work toward healing.

Plan for the Future

Consider your long-term goals and how to achieve them. This might involve making plans to leave the abusive relationship, pursuing personal or professional growth, and rebuilding your support network. Focusing on the future can provide hope and motivation to take action.

Emma's Journey to Freedom

Emma had been in a relationship with her partner, Alex, for five years. Over time, Alex's behavior became increasingly controlling and manipulative. He often criticized Emma's appearance, belittled her achievements, and isolated her from friends and family. Emma began to feel worthless and trapped, doubting her own perceptions and blaming herself for the problems in the relationship.

One day, Emma confided in her close friend, Sarah, about her experiences. Sarah listened empathetically and validated Emma's feelings, helping her recognize the signs of emotional abuse. Encouraged by Sarah's support, Emma began to document the incidents of abuse and seek information on emotional abuse and manipulation.

With Sarah's help, Emma established clear boundaries with Alex and sought therapy to rebuild her self-esteem and confidence. Her therapist provided her with tools to cope with the effects of the abuse and helped her develop a safety plan in case the situation escalated.

Over time, Emma gained the strength to leave the abusive relationship and rebuild her life. She reconnected with friends and family, pursued her career goals, and continued therapy to support her healing journey. Emma's story is a testament to the power of awareness, support, and self-empowerment in overcoming emotional abuse.

The Path to Healing and Empowerment

Emotional abuse is a deeply damaging and pervasive form of abuse that can leave lasting scars on its victims. By understanding the various types of emotional abuse, recognizing its impact, and taking proactive steps to address it, individuals can reclaim their lives and foster healthier, more empowering relationships.

Recognizing the signs of emotional abuse and seeking support are crucial steps in this journey. Establishing boundaries, practicing self-care, and considering professional help can further empower individuals to confront and overcome emotional abuse. Through awareness, education, and support, victims of emotional abuse can begin to heal and rebuild their lives, finding strength and resilience in the face of adversity.

Ultimately, the journey to healing and empowerment is a personal and ongoing process. By taking proactive steps to address emotional abuse, individuals can reclaim their sense of self-worth, build healthier relationships, and create a future free from the damaging effects of manipulation and control.

Chapter 4

Gaslighting: Understanding and Overcoming Psychological Manipulation

The Dark Art of Gaslighting

Gaslighting is one of the most insidious forms of psychological manipulation. It is a deliberate and cunning tactic used to distort the victim's perception of reality, making them question their memories, judgment, and sanity. Unlike overt forms of abuse, gaslighting is subtle, making it difficult to recognize and address. This looks into the definition and characteristics of gaslighting, its devastating effects on mental health, and strategies for overcoming this form of manipulation.

Characteristics of Gaslighting

Gaslighting is a form of psychological manipulation where the abuser seeks to sow seeds of doubt in the victim's mind, making them question their perception of reality, memory, and sanity. The term originates from the 1938 play "Gas Light" and its subsequent film adaptations, where a husband manipulates his wife into believing she is going insane by altering small elements of their environment and insisting she is mistaken or delusional when she notices the changes.

Persistent Denial and Contradiction

One of the primary tactics of gaslighting involves the persistent denial of events, statements, or actions that the victim knows to be true. The gaslighter may flatly deny having said or done something, even when there is clear evidence to the contrary. By consistently contradicting the victim, the gaslighter creates confusion and self-doubt.

Trivializing the Victim's Feelings

Gaslighters often dismiss or belittle the victim's feelings, making them feel insignificant or overly sensitive. Phrases like "You're overreacting" or "You're being too sensitive" are commonly used to undermine the victim's emotions and experiences. This tactic diminishes the victim's confidence in their own feelings and perceptions.

Using Confusion to Weaken the Victim

Creating confusion is a key element of gaslighting. The gaslighter may provide conflicting information, change stories, or shift blame in ways that leave the victim bewildered and disoriented. By keeping the victim off balance, the gaslighter maintains control and power over them.

Isolating the Victim

Gaslighters often isolate their victims from friends, family, and other support networks. By cutting off these connections, the gaslighter ensures that the victim has fewer sources of validation and support, making them more reliant on the abuser. Isolation also prevents the victim from gaining perspective on their situation.

Manipulating the Environment

Subtle manipulations of the environment are another hallmark of gaslighting. The gaslighter may move or hide objects, alter details, or create scenarios that make the victim question their memory and perception. When the victim notices these changes, the gaslighter denies any alterations, further destabilizing the victim's sense of reality.

Projection and Deflection

Gaslighters often project their own faults and behaviors onto the victim, accusing them of the very things the gaslighter is doing. This tactic deflects attention away from the gaslighter's actions and shifts blame onto the victim, creating further confusion and self-doubt.

Effects of Gaslighting on Mental Health

The effects of gaslighting on mental health are profound and long-lasting. Victims of gaslighting experience a range of psychological and emotional consequences that can severely impact their well-being.

Erosion of Self-Confidence and Self-Esteem

Gaslighting systematically erodes the victim's self-confidence and self-esteem. Constant denial, contradiction, and trivialization of the victim's experiences lead them to question their worth and capabilities. Over time, the victim internalizes the gaslighter's negative messages, believing themselves to be incompetent, untrustworthy, and inadequate.

Chronic Anxiety and Depression

The relentless nature of gaslighting creates an environment of chronic stress and anxiety. Victims often feel on edge, constantly second-guessing themselves and their perceptions. This persistent state of anxiety can lead to depression, characterized by feelings of hopelessness, helplessness, and deep sadness.

Disorientation and Confusion

Gaslighting leaves victims in a constant state of disorientation and confusion. The manipulative tactics employed by the gaslighter make it difficult for the victim to trust their own memories and judgments. This cognitive dissonance creates a sense of mental fog, where the victim struggles to make sense of their reality.

Isolation and Loneliness

The isolation imposed by the gaslighter exacerbates the victim's feelings of loneliness and abandonment. Cut off from supportive relationships and external validation, the victim becomes increasingly dependent on the gaslighter for affirmation and connection. This dependency further entrenches the victim in the cycle of abuse.

Trauma and Post-Traumatic Stress Disorder (PTSD)

The psychological manipulation and emotional abuse inherent in gaslighting can lead to trauma and PTSD. Victims may experience flashbacks, nightmares, hypervigilance, and other symptoms associated with traumatic stress. The emotional scars left by gaslighting can persist long after the abusive relationship has ended.

Strategies for Overcoming Gaslighting Tactics

Recognizing and overcoming gaslighting requires a multifaceted approach that involves self-awareness, support, and strategic action. The following strategies can help victims reclaim their reality and break free from the cycle of manipulation.

Validate Your Feelings and Experiences

One of the most important steps in overcoming gaslighting is to validate your own feelings and experiences. Trust your instincts and acknowledge that your perceptions are real and valid. Keep a journal to document specific incidents of gaslighting, noting dates, times, and details. This record can serve as a tangible reminder of your reality.

Seek External Validation and Support

Reaching out for external validation and support is crucial in counteracting the effects of gaslighting. Share your experiences with trusted friends, family members, or a mental health professional. Their perspectives can help reinforce your sense of reality and provide much-needed emotional support.

Establish Boundaries

Setting and enforcing boundaries with the gaslighter is essential for protecting yourself from further manipulation. Clearly communicate your limits and assertively maintain them. This may involve limiting contact, refusing to engage in manipulative conversations, or seeking physical separation if necessary.

Educate Yourself About Gaslighting

Knowledge is a powerful tool in combating gaslighting. Educate yourself about the tactics and characteristics of gaslighting through books, articles, and reputable resources. Understanding the dynamics of gaslighting can help you recognize and resist manipulative behaviors.

Build Self-Confidence and Self-Esteem

Rebuilding your self-confidence and self-esteem is a critical part of recovering from gaslighting. Engage in activities that promote self-affirmation and personal growth. Practice self-compassion and challenge negative self-talk. Surround yourself with positive influences that uplift and support you.

Develop a Support Network

Creating a strong support network is vital for overcoming gaslighting. Connect with supportive friends, family members, and community resources. Join support groups or online forums where you can share your experiences and gain insights from others who have faced similar challenges.

Practice Self-Care

Prioritizing self-care is essential for healing from the effects of gaslighting. Engage in activities that promote relaxation, well-being, and joy. This can include exercise, hobbies, meditation, and spending time in nature. Self-care helps to replenish your emotional reserves and strengthen your resilience.

Consider Professional Help

Therapy can be an invaluable resource for overcoming gaslighting. A mental health professional can provide a safe space to process your experiences, develop coping strategies, and rebuild your sense of self. Therapeutic approaches such as cognitive-behavioral therapy (CBT) can help challenge distorted thinking patterns and reinforce healthy self-perception.

Plan for Safety and Exit Strategies

If you are in a relationship with a gaslighter, planning for safety and exit strategies is crucial. Identify safe places to go, keep important documents and emergency contacts accessible, and have a plan for leaving the relationship if necessary. Your safety and well-being are paramount.

Mark's Path to Clarity

Mark had been in a relationship with his partner, Lisa, for several years. Over time, he began to notice that Lisa would often deny events, twist facts, and make him feel confused and unsure of himself. She would frequently tell him that he was "imagining things" or "being paranoid." Mark found himself questioning his memory and judgment, feeling increasingly disoriented and anxious.

One day, Mark confided in his sister about his experiences. She listened attentively and suggested that he might be experiencing gaslighting. With her encouragement, Mark began to keep a journal of specific incidents and his feelings. This documentation helped him see the patterns of manipulation more clearly.

Mark sought the help of a therapist, who provided him with tools to rebuild his self-confidence and challenge the gaslighting tactics. Through therapy, Mark learned to trust his own perceptions and validate his feelings. He also established firm boundaries with Lisa and limited their interactions.

Eventually, Mark decided to end the relationship and focus on his healing journey. He reconnected with friends and family, pursued his interests, and continued therapy. Mark's story illustrates the importance of self-awareness, support, and professional help in overcoming gaslighting.

Reclaiming Your Reality

Gaslighting is a powerful and destructive form of psychological manipulation that can leave deep emotional scars. By understanding its characteristics, recognizing its impact, and implementing strategies to counteract it, individuals can reclaim their sense of reality and break free from the cycle of manipulation.

Validating your feelings, seeking support, and establishing boundaries are crucial steps in this journey. Educating yourself about gaslighting, practicing self-care, and considering professional help can further empower you to overcome this insidious form of abuse.

Ultimately, the path to recovery from gaslighting is one of self-discovery and empowerment. By trusting yourself, building resilience, and surrounding yourself with positive influences, you can reclaim your reality and move forward with strength and clarity.

Chapter 5

Types of Manipulative Personalities

Manipulative personalities can be found in various walks of life, often masking their true intentions behind charming or unassuming facades. Understanding the different types of manipulators, their behavior patterns, and the red flags can help individuals protect themselves from emotional and psychological harm. It explores the profiles of different manipulative personalities, the common behaviors they exhibit, and real-life case studies that highlight their tactics.

The Charismatic Manipulator

The charismatic manipulator is often charming, articulate, and appears confident and likable. These individuals use their charisma to win trust and admiration, making it difficult for others to believe they could have ulterior motives. They thrive in social situations, using their charm to influence and control those around them.

Behavior Patterns and Red Flags Charismatic manipulators are skilled at making others feel special and valued. They often use flattery and compliments to gain trust and create a sense of loyalty. However, they may also exhibit a pattern of inconsistent behavior, such as being overly attentive one moment and distant the next. This creates confusion and dependency in their targets.

They may also exploit their charisma to manipulate group dynamics, turning people against each other to maintain control. They are adept at deflecting blame and can make their victims feel responsible for any issues that arise.

The Charming Leader

Jessica was known for her charismatic leadership in her community. She was always the center of attention at social gatherings and had a way of making people feel important. However, beneath her charm, Jessica had a habit of manipulating those around her. She would promise opportunities and favors to her followers but rarely followed through. Instead, she used these promises to keep people loyal and dependent on her. When confronted, Jessica would use her charm to deflect blame, making her victims doubt their own perceptions.

The Victim Manipulator

Victim manipulators present themselves as helpless or oppressed, using sympathy and guilt to control others. They often create scenarios where they appear to be the victim of circumstances, eliciting pity and support from those around them. This type of manipulation can be particularly effective as it plays on the natural human inclination to help those in need.

Behavior Patterns and Red Flags

Victim manipulators often tell stories of their misfortunes and hardships, exaggerating or fabricating details to gain sympathy. They may frequently seek help or favors, making their supporters feel guilty for not assisting. These individuals rarely take responsibility for their actions, always finding someone or something else to blame for their problems.

Another red flag is their tendency to create drama and crisis situations, ensuring they remain the focus of attention and support. They often isolate their targets from others who might see through their manipulation, reinforcing their dependency.

The Perpetual Victim

Tom was always in need of help. Whether it was financial support, emotional comfort, or assistance with daily tasks, he consistently turned to his friends and family for aid. He told elaborate stories of betrayal and bad luck, making those around him feel sorry for him. However, whenever someone tried to help him find long-term solutions, Tom would resist, preferring to remain in his victim role. Over time, his friends began to notice the pattern and realized that Tom was using their sympathy to manipulate them.

The Narcissistic Manipulator

Narcissistic manipulators are driven by a deep need for admiration and validation. They often have an inflated sense of self-importance and a lack of empathy for others. These individuals use manipulation to maintain their superiority and control over others, often disregarding the feelings and needs of those around them.

Behavior Patterns and Red Flags

Narcissistic manipulators are highly self-centered and often dominate conversations, focusing on their achievements and importance. They may use others as tools to achieve their own goals, showing little regard for the impact on those they manipulate. Criticism or rejection can provoke extreme reactions, as they cannot tolerate anything that threatens their inflated self-image.

A common red flag is their tendency to belittle or demean others to assert their superiority. They may also engage in gaslighting, making their victims question their own reality and sanity. Their lack of empathy often becomes evident in their interactions, as they fail to consider the feelings and needs of others.

The Self-Absorbed Partner

Rachel was in a relationship with David, who seemed charming and successful at first. However, as the relationship progressed, Rachel noticed that David was extremely self-centered. He constantly talked about his achievements and dismissed Rachel's feelings and concerns. Whenever Rachel tried to express her needs, David would belittle her, making her feel insignificant. He would also manipulate situations to make Rachel doubt her own perceptions, causing her to question her sanity. Over time, Rachel realized that David's behavior was a pattern of narcissistic manipulation and sought help to break free from the toxic relationship.

The Passive-Aggressive Manipulator

Passive-aggressive manipulators express their hostility and resistance indirectly, often using subtle and covert tactics to control others. They may avoid direct confrontation, instead opting for behaviors that confuse and frustrate their targets. This form of manipulation can be particularly damaging as it is difficult to identify and address.

Behavior Patterns and Red Flags

Passive-aggressive manipulators often exhibit a pattern of procrastination, deliberate inefficiency, and stubbornness. They may agree to requests or commitments but then sabotage their own efforts, ensuring failure. This allows them to maintain a facade of cooperation while expressing their underlying resistance and hostility.

Red flags include frequent excuses, blame-shifting, and playing the victim when confronted. They may also use sarcasm, backhanded compliments, and subtle put-downs to undermine others. Their indirect approach makes it challenging to address the manipulation directly, as they can easily deny any ill intent.

The Subtle Saboteur

Emma worked with a colleague, Mike, who was notorious for his passive-aggressive behavior. Mike would agree to take on tasks but then consistently miss deadlines and produce subpar work. When confronted, he would make excuses and play the victim, claiming he was overwhelmed or misunderstood the instructions. He also used sarcasm and subtle insults to undermine Emma's confidence and credibility. Recognizing the pattern, Emma documented Mike's behavior and sought support from her supervisor to address the issue.

The Controlling Manipulator

Controlling manipulators exert power and dominance over others, often using fear, intimidation, and coercion. They seek to control every aspect of their target's life, including their thoughts, actions, and decisions. This form of manipulation can be overt and aggressive, leaving the victim feeling powerless and trapped.

Behavior Patterns and Red Flags

Controlling manipulators often use threats, intimidation, and verbal abuse to maintain control. They may monitor their target's activities, isolate them from support networks, and enforce rigid rules and expectations. Any deviation from their control can provoke extreme anger and punitive actions.

Red flags include a pattern of dominance and authoritarian behavior, a lack of respect for boundaries, and a refusal to allow independence or autonomy. They may also exhibit possessiveness and jealousy, using these emotions to justify their controlling actions.

The Dominant Spouse

Sara was married to John, who exhibited controlling behavior from the beginning of their relationship. John insisted on knowing every detail of Sara's day, monitored her phone and social media, and restricted her interactions with friends and family. He used threats and intimidation to enforce his rules, making Sara feel trapped and powerless. Recognizing the abuse, Sara reached out to a support group and developed a plan to safely leave the relationship and regain her independence.

The Opportunistic Manipulator

Opportunistic manipulators are driven by self-interest and will exploit any situation or person to achieve their goals. They are highly adaptable and can switch tactics and behaviors based on what benefits them the most. This form of manipulation is often seen in professional settings, where individuals use deceit and cunning to advance their careers or personal agendas.

Behavior Patterns and Red Flags

Opportunistic manipulators are highly strategic and can appear cooperative and charming when it serves their purpose. They are skilled at identifying weaknesses and opportunities, using this knowledge to their advantage. They may engage in deceptive practices, such as lying, cheating, and backstabbing, to achieve their goals.

Red flags include a pattern of opportunistic behavior, inconsistency in actions and words, and a lack of genuine loyalty or integrity. They may also exhibit a high level of competitiveness and a willingness to sacrifice others for their own gain.

The Ambitious Colleague

Mark worked in a competitive corporate environment and had a colleague, Lisa, who seemed friendly and supportive. However, Mark began to notice that Lisa would often take credit for his ideas, spread rumors about him, and manipulate situations to her advantage. She was highly strategic and would switch alliances based on who could benefit her the most. Recognizing Lisa's opportunistic behavior, Mark documented her actions and sought mentorship to navigate the workplace dynamics more effectively.

The Seductive Manipulator

Seductive manipulators use charm, flattery, and often physical attractiveness to manipulate others. They exploit emotional and romantic vulnerabilities, creating a sense of intimacy and connection to achieve their goals. This form of manipulation can be particularly powerful as it taps into deep emotional and psychological needs.

Behavior Patterns and Red Flags

Seductive manipulators are highly skilled at creating a sense of attraction and connection. They use flattery, compliments, and romantic gestures to win trust and affection. However, they may also exhibit patterns of inconsistency, such as intense interest followed by sudden withdrawal, creating confusion and dependency.

Red flags include a pattern of using charm and attractiveness to achieve goals, a lack of genuine emotional depth, and a tendency to manipulate emotions and affections. They may also engage in triangulation, using other relationships to create jealousy and competition.

The Charming Romantic

Anna met Jack, who seemed like the perfect partner. He was charming, attentive, and made her feel special. However, Anna began to notice that Jack would often withdraw his affection abruptly, leaving her feeling confused and insecure. He also used flattery and charm to manipulate her into doing things she was uncomfortable with. Recognizing the pattern, Anna sought support from friends and realized that Jack was using seductive manipulation to control her.

The Martyr Manipulator

Martyr manipulators present themselves as self-sacrificing and long-suffering, using their perceived suffering to control and manipulate others. They often guilt-trip their targets into compliance by emphasizing their own sacrifices and hardships. This form of manipulation can create a sense of obligation and indebtedness in the victim.

Behavior Patterns and Red Flags

Martyr manipulators frequently highlight their sacrifices and struggles, making others feel guilty for not recognizing or appreciating their efforts. They may use phrases like "After everything I've done for you" to manipulate their targets into compliance. They also have a tendency to take on a victim role, seeking sympathy and support.

Red flags include a pattern of emphasizing sacrifices and hardships, using guilt to manipulate, and a tendency to take on a victim role. They may also resist any attempts to help or change their situation, preferring to remain in their martyr role.

The Self-Sacrificing Parent

Emily's mother, Karen, was always emphasizing the sacrifices she had made for her children. She frequently reminded Emily of the hardships she had endured and used guilt to manipulate Emily into doing things for her. Karen would say things like, "After everything I've done for you, you can't even do this one thing for me?" Recognizing the pattern, Emily sought therapy to address the emotional manipulation and set boundaries with her mother.

The Calculating Manipulator

Calculating manipulators are highly strategic and methodical in their approach. They plan their actions carefully, considering the long-term consequences and benefits. This type of manipulation is often seen in competitive environments, where individuals use their intelligence and cunning to outmaneuver others.

Behavior Patterns and Red Flags

Calculating manipulators exhibit a high level of strategic thinking and planning. They often have a clear agenda and use manipulation as a means to achieve their goals. They are skilled at hiding their true intentions and can be very patient, waiting for the right moment to strike.

Red flags include a pattern of strategic thinking and planning, a lack of transparency, and a tendency to manipulate situations and people for their own gain. They may also exhibit a high level of patience and cunning, making it difficult to detect their manipulation.

The Strategic Executive

David was an executive in a large corporation and had a colleague, John, who was known for his strategic thinking. John would carefully plan his actions, manipulating situations and people to achieve his goals. He would often withhold information, create alliances, and sabotage competitors. Recognizing John's calculating behavior, David documented his actions and sought support from senior management to address the issue.

The Sadistic Manipulator

Sadistic manipulators derive pleasure from causing pain and suffering to others. They use manipulation to exert control and inflict harm, often enjoying the power they have over their victims. This form of manipulation is particularly harmful as it involves intentional cruelty and abuse.

Behavior Patterns and Red Flags

Sadistic manipulators exhibit a pattern of cruelty and abuse, often using manipulation to inflict pain and suffering. They may use verbal, emotional, or physical abuse to control their victims. They also exhibit a lack of empathy and a tendency to enjoy the suffering of others.

Red flags include a pattern of cruelty and abuse, a lack of empathy, and a tendency to enjoy the suffering of others. They may also exhibit a high level of control and dominance, making it difficult for their victims to escape the abuse.

The Abusive Partner

Laura was in a relationship with Tom, who exhibited sadistic behavior. Tom would manipulate Laura through verbal and emotional abuse, enjoying the power he had over her. He would belittle her, isolate her from friends and family, and use threats and intimidation to maintain control. Recognizing the abuse, Laura sought help from a domestic violence support group and developed a plan to safely leave the relationship.

The Envious Manipulator

Envious manipulators are driven by jealousy and resentment. They manipulate others to bring them down and elevate themselves, often engaging in sabotage and deceit. This form of manipulation is fueled by a desire to undermine others and take what they have.

Behavior Patterns and Red Flags

Envious manipulators exhibit a pattern of jealousy and resentment, often targeting those they perceive as threats. They may engage in sabotage, spreading rumors, and deceit to undermine their targets. They also exhibit a lack of genuine support and loyalty, as their actions are driven by envy.

Red flags include a pattern of jealousy and resentment, sabotage and deceit, and a lack of genuine support and loyalty. They may also exhibit a high level of competitiveness, always seeking to undermine their targets.

The Jealous Colleague

Sarah worked with a colleague, Amy, who exhibited envious behavior. Amy would frequently undermine Sarah's work, spread rumors about her, and take credit for her ideas. She was driven by jealousy and resentment, always seeking to bring Sarah down. Recognizing Amy's envious behavior, Sarah documented her actions and sought support from her supervisor to address the issue.

The Guilt-Tripping Manipulator

Guilt-tripping manipulators use guilt and shame to control others. They often highlight their own suffering and sacrifices, making their targets feel responsible for their well-being. This form of manipulation creates a sense of obligation and indebtedness in the victim.

Behavior Patterns and Red Flags

Guilt-tripping manipulators frequently emphasize their own suffering and sacrifices, using guilt and shame to manipulate others. They may use phrases like "You owe me" or "After everything I've done for you" to control their targets. They also exhibit a pattern of taking on a victim role, seeking sympathy and support.

Red flags include a pattern of emphasizing suffering and sacrifices, using guilt and shame to manipulate, and a tendency to take on a victim role. They may also resist any attempts to help or change their situation, preferring to remain in their guilt-tripping role.

The Manipulative Friend

Tom had a friend, Mike, who frequently used guilt-tripping to manipulate him. Mike would often remind Tom of the favors he had done for him and use phrases like "You owe me" to control him. He would also emphasize his own suffering and sacrifices, making Tom feel guilty for not helping him. Recognizing the pattern, Tom set boundaries with Mike and sought support from other friends to address the manipulation.

The Intimidating Manipulator

Intimidating manipulators use fear and threats to control others. They often exhibit aggressive and domineering behavior, using their power to manipulate and control their targets. This form of manipulation creates a sense of fear and helplessness in the victim.

Behavior Patterns and Red Flags

Intimidating manipulators exhibit a pattern of aggressive and domineering behavior. They use threats, intimidation, and verbal abuse to maintain control. They also exhibit a lack of respect for boundaries and a refusal to allow independence or autonomy.

Red flags include a pattern of aggression and domination, a lack of respect for boundaries, and a refusal to allow independence or autonomy. They may also exhibit possessiveness and jealousy, using these emotions to justify their intimidating actions.

The Bullying Boss

Jane worked for a boss, Mark, who exhibited intimidating behavior. Mark would use threats and verbal abuse to control his employees, making them feel fearful and helpless. He would also monitor their activities and restrict their autonomy, creating a sense of domination and control. Recognizing the abuse, Jane documented Mark's behavior and sought support from HR to address the issue.

The Emotional Manipulator

Emotional manipulators use emotions to control and manipulate others. They often exploit their targets' feelings, using guilt, shame, and sympathy to achieve their goals. This form of manipulation creates a sense of emotional confusion and dependency in the victim.

Behavior Patterns and Red Flags

Emotional manipulators exhibit a pattern of exploiting emotions to manipulate others. They may use guilt, shame, and sympathy to control their targets. They also exhibit a lack of genuine emotional depth and a tendency to manipulate emotions and affections.

Red flags include a pattern of using emotions to manipulate, a lack of genuine emotional depth, and a tendency to manipulate emotions and affections. They may also engage in triangulation, using other relationships to create jealousy and competition.

The Manipulative Partner

Laura was in a relationship with Tom, who exhibited emotional manipulation. Tom would often use guilt and shame to control Laura, making her feel responsible for his well-being. He would also exploit her emotions, using sympathy and affection to manipulate her. Recognizing the pattern, Laura sought support from friends and realized that Tom was using emotional manipulation to control her.

The Self-Centered Manipulator

Self-centered manipulators are highly focused on their own needs and desires. They use manipulation to achieve their goals, often disregarding the feelings and needs of others. This form of manipulation is characterized by a lack of empathy and a tendency to use others as tools to achieve their own ends.

Behavior Patterns and Red Flags

Self-centered manipulators exhibit a pattern of self-centered behavior and a lack of empathy. They often use others as tools to achieve their goals, showing little regard for the impact on those they manipulate. They may also exhibit a high level of entitlement and a tendency to dominate conversations and interactions.

Red flags include a pattern of self-centered behavior, a lack of empathy, and a tendency to use others as tools. They may also exhibit a high level of entitlement and a tendency to dominate conversations and interactions.

The Self-Absorbed Colleague

Rachel worked with a colleague, David, who exhibited self-centered behavior. David would often dominate conversations, focusing on his achievements and importance. He would also use others as tools to achieve his goals, showing little regard for their feelings and needs. Recognizing David's self-centered behavior, Rachel sought support from her supervisor to address the issue.

Understanding the various types of manipulative personalities and their behavior patterns can help individuals recognize and address manipulation in their lives. By being aware of the red flags and the tactics used by manipulators, individuals can protect themselves and maintain healthy, strong relationships.

Chapter 6

Challenges Victims Face: Breaking Free from Manipulative Relationships

Breaking free from manipulative relationships is one of the most daunting and painful journeys one can undertake. The victims of such relationships often face a multitude of challenges that can make the process of leaving seem insurmountable. It looks into the barriers to leaving abusive relationships, the emotional and psychological hurdles victims must overcome, and the support systems and resources available to aid them in their journey toward freedom and healing.

Barriers to Leaving Abusive Relationships

One of the most significant barriers to leaving a manipulative relationship is the fear of the unknown. Victims often become so entrenched in the toxic dynamics that the idea of life outside the relationship feels terrifying and uncertain. This fear is compounded by the manipulator's tactics, which frequently include threats of harm or abandonment if the victim attempts to leave.

Manipulators may also isolate their victims from friends and family, making it difficult for them to seek help or even recognize that help is available. This isolation reinforces the victim's belief that they have nowhere to turn.

Financial dependence is another critical barrier. Many manipulative individuals exert control over their victims by restricting their access to money, making them financially dependent. This financial control can create a sense of helplessness, as victims may not have the resources to support themselves if they leave. The fear of economic instability can be paralyzing, particularly if the victim has children or other dependents to care for.

Social stigma and shame also play a significant role in preventing victims from leaving. Society often judges victims harshly, questioning why they stayed in the relationship or blaming them for the abuse. This judgment can lead to deep feelings of shame and guilt, making it even harder for victims to seek help. Additionally, victims may fear not being believed or taken seriously, especially if the manipulative individual is charismatic or well-respected in the community.

Emotional and Psychological Challenges for Victims

The emotional and psychological challenges faced by victims of manipulative relationships are profound. One of the most pervasive is the erosion of self-esteem and self-worth. Manipulative individuals often use tactics like gaslighting to undermine their victims' confidence and make them doubt their perceptions and reality. Over time, this can lead to a significant loss of self-esteem, making it difficult for victims to believe they deserve better or have the strength to leave.

The trauma bond is another significant challenge. Trauma bonding occurs when the victim develops a strong emotional attachment to the manipulator due to intermittent reinforcement of abuse and kindness. This cycle of abuse followed by periods of affection creates a powerful and confusing attachment that is hard to break. Victims may find themselves rationalizing the manipulator's behavior, believing that the moments of kindness outweigh the abuse, or hoping that the abuser will change.

Depression and anxiety are common among victims of manipulative relationships. The constant stress and fear take a toll on mental health, leading to feelings of hopelessness and despair. Victims may struggle with anxiety about the future, worrying about their safety and the potential repercussions of leaving. This anxiety can be overwhelming, making it difficult to take action or make clear decisions.

Additionally, victims often experience a deep sense of loss and grief when considering leaving the relationship. Despite the abuse, there may have been genuine moments of connection and love that make the idea of leaving feel like a betrayal of those good times. This conflict between the desire for safety and the emotional attachment to the manipulator creates a painful internal struggle.

Support Systems and Resources Available for Victims

Despite the numerous challenges, there are support systems and resources available to help victims break free from manipulative relationships. Recognizing that they are not alone and that help is available is a crucial first step for victims.

One of the most valuable resources is counseling and therapy. Professional counselors and therapists who specialize in abuse and trauma can provide a safe space for victims to process their experiences and develop coping strategies. Therapy can help rebuild self-esteem, address trauma, and create a plan for leaving the relationship safely. Group therapy or support groups can also be beneficial, as they allow victims to connect with others who have had similar experiences and gain strength from shared stories of survival and resilience.

Hotlines and crisis centers offer immediate support for victims in need. Organizations such as the National Domestic Violence Hotline provide 24/7 assistance, offering confidential support and connecting victims to local resources. These hotlines can be a lifeline for those who feel isolated and unsure of where to turn.

Shelters and safe houses provide a temporary refuge for victims who need to leave their homes quickly. These facilities offer a safe and supportive environment where victims can access basic needs, legal assistance, and emotional support. Many shelters also provide resources for children, ensuring that the entire family is supported during the transition.

Legal assistance is another crucial resource. Many victims of manipulative relationships face legal challenges, whether it's obtaining restraining orders, navigating custody disputes, or seeking a divorce. Legal aid organizations and pro bono attorneys can provide the necessary legal support to help victims protect themselves and their rights.

Community organizations and advocacy groups play a vital role in supporting victims. These groups often offer a range of services, including education, advocacy, and direct support. They work to raise awareness about the issue of manipulation and abuse, advocate for policy changes, and provide direct assistance to those in need.

Friends and family can also be a powerful source of support. Reaching out to trusted loved ones can provide emotional backing and practical assistance. It's important for friends and family to listen without judgment, offer a safe space, and help the victim explore their options.

In addition to these resources, online platforms and forums can offer valuable information and support. Websites dedicated to abuse survivors provide educational materials, personal stories, and forums where victims can share their experiences and seek advice. These online communities can offer a sense of solidarity and understanding that is crucial for healing.

Breaking free from a manipulative relationship is an incredibly challenging and courageous journey. Victims face numerous barriers, from fear and financial dependence to social stigma and emotional attachment. The psychological toll of such relationships is profound, leaving victims with shattered self-esteem, trauma bonds, and mental health struggles. However, hope and help are available. Through counseling, hotlines, shelters, legal assistance, and support from loved ones and community organizations, victims can find the strength and resources they need to reclaim their lives. The path to freedom and healing is not easy, but it is possible, and taking that first step is the beginning of a new, healthier, and more empowering chapter

Chapter 7

Developing Self-Awareness: Understanding Your Vulnerabilities

Self-awareness is a cornerstone of personal growth and emotional health. For those who have experienced manipulative relationships, developing self-awareness is crucial in understanding their vulnerabilities, building emotional resilience, and enhancing self-protection. It therefore explores the process of reflecting on personal weaknesses that can be exploited, the importance of building emotional resilience and self-esteem, and techniques for enhancing self-awareness and self-protection.

Reflecting on Personal Weaknesses That Can Be Exploited

Understanding and reflecting on personal weaknesses is a vital step in developing self-awareness. Everyone has vulnerabilities, and manipulative individuals are adept at identifying and exploiting these weaknesses. To protect oneself, it is essential to recognize these potential pitfalls and address them proactively.

One common vulnerability is the need for validation and approval from others. Many people derive a sense of self-worth from external sources, seeking affirmation and acceptance to feel valued. Manipulators often exploit this need by offering praise and attention initially, creating a dependency on their approval. Once this dependency is established, they can manipulate the victim's emotions by withholding approval or offering criticism.

Another exploitable weakness is the fear of conflict and desire to maintain peace. Individuals who avoid confrontation and prioritize harmony may find themselves acquiescing to unreasonable demands to avoid discord. Manipulators use this to their advantage by pushing boundaries, knowing the victim is unlikely to push back. This pattern of behavior can erode the victim's sense of agency and reinforce the manipulator's control.

Low self-esteem and self-doubt are also significant vulnerabilities. People who struggle with self-worth may be more susceptible to manipulation, as they may believe they do not deserve better treatment or that the manipulator's negative assessments are accurate. This internalized negative self-view can make it challenging to recognize manipulation and take steps to address it.

Reflecting on these and other personal weaknesses involves honest introspection. It requires acknowledging areas where one may be susceptible to manipulation and understanding how these vulnerabilities have been exploited in the past. This reflection is not about self-blame but about gaining insight into one's emotional landscape to build stronger defenses.

Building Emotional Resilience and Self-Esteem

Building emotional resilience and self-esteem is crucial in protecting oneself from manipulation. Emotional resilience is the ability to adapt to stressful situations and recover from adversity. It involves developing a strong internal foundation that can withstand external pressures and manipulative tactics.

One way to build emotional resilience is through self-compassion. Self-compassion involves treating oneself with kindness and understanding during difficult times, rather than with self-criticism. By practicing self-compassion, individuals can cultivate a sense of inner strength and stability. This practice helps to create a supportive inner dialogue that counteracts the negative messages from manipulators.

Another aspect of emotional resilience is developing healthy coping mechanisms. This can include mindfulness practices, such as meditation and deep breathing, which help manage stress and maintain emotional equilibrium.

Engaging in activities that bring joy and fulfillment, such as hobbies or physical exercise, can also enhance emotional resilience by providing positive outlets for stress and reinforcing a sense of self-worth.

Building self-esteem involves recognizing and valuing one's inherent worth and abilities. This process often requires challenging negative self-beliefs and replacing them with positive affirmations. Setting and achieving small, manageable goals can help build confidence and reinforce a sense of accomplishment. Surrounding oneself with supportive and affirming people can also play a significant role in bolstering self-esteem.

Therapy or counseling can be instrumental in building emotional resilience and self-esteem. A trained therapist can help individuals explore the roots of their vulnerabilities, develop healthy coping strategies, and build a stronger sense of self. Group therapy or support groups can also provide a sense of community and shared understanding, which can be incredibly empowering.

Techniques for Enhancing Self-Awareness and Self-Protection

Enhancing self-awareness and self-protection requires intentional effort and the adoption of specific techniques designed to foster a deeper understanding of oneself and build defenses against manipulation.

One effective technique for enhancing self-awareness is journaling. Writing regularly about one's thoughts, feelings, and experiences can provide valuable insights into patterns of behavior and emotional responses. Journaling can help individuals identify triggers for their vulnerabilities and recognize how manipulators have exploited them in the past. This increased awareness can empower individuals to make more conscious choices and set healthier boundaries.

Mindfulness practices are another powerful tool for enhancing self-awareness. Mindfulness involves paying attention to the present moment without judgment. By practicing mindfulness, individuals can develop a greater awareness of their thoughts, feelings, and bodily sensations. This heightened awareness can help them recognize when they are being manipulated and respond more effectively. Techniques such as meditation, body scanning, and mindful breathing can be incorporated into daily routines to cultivate mindfulness.

Setting clear and firm boundaries is a critical aspect of self-protection. Boundaries define what is acceptable and unacceptable behavior and help protect one's emotional and physical well-being. Establishing boundaries requires a strong sense of self-worth and the ability to assert one's needs and limits. Practicing assertive communication can be beneficial in this regard. Assertive communication involves expressing oneself clearly and respectfully, without aggression or passivity. It empowers individuals to stand up for themselves and enforce their boundaries.

Education and knowledge are also essential components of self-protection. Understanding the tactics that manipulators use and the dynamics of manipulative relationships can provide individuals with the tools to recognize and counteract manipulation. Reading books, attending workshops, or participating in online courses on topics such as emotional abuse, gaslighting, and psychological manipulation can enhance one's understanding and preparedness.

Building a strong support network is another crucial element of self-protection. Trusted friends, family members, and support groups can provide validation, encouragement, and practical assistance. Having a network of supportive individuals can help counteract the isolation that manipulators often impose and provide a sounding board for one's experiences and decisions.

Developing emotional intelligence is another valuable technique for enhancing self-awareness and self-protection. Emotional intelligence involves the ability to understand and manage one's emotions and the emotions of others. By developing emotional intelligence, individuals can better navigate their relationships and recognize manipulative behaviors. This can be achieved through practices such as active listening, empathy, and reflective thinking.

Regular self-reflection is also important for maintaining self-awareness and self-protection. Taking time to reflect on one's experiences, emotions, and behaviors can provide ongoing insights and help individuals stay attuned to their needs and boundaries. This can be done through activities such as meditation, yoga, or simply taking quiet moments for contemplation.

Developing self-awareness is a transformative journey that involves understanding one's vulnerabilities, building emotional resilience and self-esteem, and adopting techniques for self-protection. By reflecting on personal weaknesses and recognizing how they have been exploited, individuals can gain valuable insights into their emotional landscape. Building emotional resilience and self-esteem provides a strong foundation for resisting manipulation and fostering a sense of inner strength. Techniques such as journaling, mindfulness, boundary setting, education, building a support network, developing emotional intelligence, and regular self-reflection can enhance self-awareness and provide robust defenses against manipulation. Through this journey of self-discovery and growth, individuals can empower themselves to break free from manipulative relationships and build healthier, more fulfilling lives.

Chapter 8

Empowerment Strategies: Tools for Setting Boundaries

Setting and maintaining boundaries is essential for preserving one's well-being and self-respect, particularly when dealing with manipulative individuals. Boundaries are the limits we establish to protect ourselves physically, emotionally, and mentally. It explores empowerment strategies for setting boundaries, including assertiveness techniques, effective communication skills, and role-playing exercises and scenarios for practicing boundary-setting.

Assertiveness Techniques for Setting and Maintaining Boundaries

Assertiveness is a vital skill in establishing and maintaining boundaries. It involves expressing one's needs, desires, and limits clearly and confidently while respecting the rights of others. Assertiveness is distinct from aggressiveness, which disregards others' rights, and passivity, which neglects one's own needs. By mastering assertiveness techniques, individuals can stand firm in their boundaries and resist manipulation.

One fundamental assertiveness technique is using "I" statements. "I" statements focus on one's feelings and needs without blaming or criticizing others. For example, instead of saying, "You never listen to me," an assertive "I" statement would be, "I feel unheard when you talk over me. I need you to listen to my perspective." This approach minimizes defensiveness and encourages constructive dialogue.

Another technique is the broken record method. This involves calmly and persistently repeating one's position or request, regardless of how the other person responds. For example, if someone pressures you to do something you're uncomfortable with, you can repeatedly say, "No, I'm not comfortable with that." The broken record method reinforces your boundary without getting drawn into lengthy arguments or justifications.

Setting limits is also crucial. Clearly defining what is acceptable and unacceptable behavior helps reinforce boundaries. For instance, if someone repeatedly disrespects your time by being late, you can set a limit by saying, "If you're more than 15 minutes late, I will leave." This sets a clear consequence for boundary violations and shows that you take your limits seriously.

Practicing self-affirmation is another important aspect of assertiveness. Reminding yourself of your worth and your right to set boundaries can bolster your confidence and resolve. Affirmations such as, "I have the right to my feelings and needs," or "My boundaries are valid and important," can reinforce a positive self-image and strengthen your assertiveness.

Effective Communication Skills in Dealing with Manipulators

Effective communication is essential when dealing with manipulators. Manipulative individuals often use communication tactics to undermine, control, or confuse their targets. By honing effective communication skills, individuals can resist manipulation and uphold their boundaries.

One key skill is active listening. Active listening involves fully focusing on the speaker, understanding their message, and responding thoughtfully. This can help identify manipulative tactics and respond appropriately. Techniques for active listening include maintaining eye contact, nodding, and providing feedback, such as summarizing what the other person has said to confirm understanding. For example, "So, you're saying that you're upset because I didn't call you back immediately?"

Nonverbal communication is also crucial. Body language, facial expressions, and tone of voice can convey confidence and assertiveness. Maintaining an open posture, making eye contact, and using a calm, steady tone can enhance the impact of your words and reinforce your boundaries.

Setting clear and specific boundaries is essential. Vague or ambiguous boundaries can be easily manipulated or ignored. For example, instead of saying, "I need more respect," be specific: "I need you to stop interrupting me when I'm speaking." Clear boundaries leave less room for manipulation and make it easier to enforce consequences.

Using neutral language can also be effective. Manipulators often try to provoke emotional reactions to gain control. Responding with neutral, non-emotional language can defuse these attempts and keep the focus on the issue at hand. For example, instead of reacting angrily to a provocative comment, calmly state, "I disagree with that," and return to the main topic.

Setting and maintaining boundaries also involves recognizing and challenging manipulative tactics. Common tactics include guilt-tripping, gaslighting, and playing the victim. By being aware of these tactics, individuals can identify when they are being manipulated and respond assertively. For example, if someone tries to guilt-trip you by saying, "You're so selfish for not helping me," respond with an assertive statement: "I understand that you're upset, but I have other commitments that I need to prioritize."

Role-Playing Exercises and Scenarios for Practicing Boundary-Setting

Role-playing exercises and scenarios are effective tools for practicing boundary-setting. These exercises allow individuals to rehearse assertiveness techniques and communication skills in a safe and controlled environment. By practicing different scenarios, individuals can build confidence and develop strategies for real-life situations.

One useful role-playing exercise is the assertiveness script. This involves creating a script for a specific situation where boundaries need to be set and then practicing the script with a partner. For example, if you need to set a boundary with a friend who frequently borrows money and doesn't repay it, you can create a script like this: "I value our friendship, but I need to talk about the money you borrowed. I need you to repay what you owe before I can lend you more." Practicing this script with a partner can help you refine your delivery and build confidence.

Another exercise is the boundary-setting scenario. In this exercise, one person plays the role of the manipulator, and the other practices setting and enforcing boundaries. For example, the manipulator might say, "If you really cared about me, you'd help me with this project," and the person practicing might respond, "I care about you, but I have other commitments right now and can't help with the project." This exercise helps individuals practice responding to common manipulative tactics and maintaining their boundaries.

The mirror exercise is another useful tool. In this exercise, individuals practice delivering assertive statements in front of a mirror. This helps them become more aware of their body language, facial expressions, and tone of voice. By observing themselves, they can make adjustments to ensure their communication is confident and assertive.

Group role-playing can also be beneficial. In a group setting, individuals can take turns practicing different scenarios and receiving feedback from others. This provides a diverse range of perspectives and suggestions, enhancing the learning experience. Group role-playing can also create a sense of community and support, which can be empowering and motivating.

Empowerment through boundary-setting is a critical aspect of personal growth and self-protection, especially when dealing with manipulative individuals. By mastering assertiveness techniques, individuals can clearly and confidently express their needs and limits. Effective communication skills, including active listening, nonverbal communication, and the use of neutral language, can help resist manipulation and uphold boundaries. Role-playing exercises and scenarios provide practical opportunities to rehearse these skills and build confidence. Through these empowerment strategies, individuals can protect their well-being, preserve their self-respect, and foster healthier, more respectful relationships.

Chapter 9

Redefining Rules of Engagement: Establishing Healthy Relationship Dynamics

Establishing healthy relationship dynamics is fundamental to fostering connections that are nurturing, respectful, and supportive. Understanding the principles of healthy relationships, recognizing red flags to avoid, and implementing strategies for promoting mutual respect and trust are essential steps in building and maintaining fulfilling relationships. It looks into these crucial aspects in detail, offering insights and practical advice for anyone seeking to create stronger, healthier bonds.

Principles of Healthy Relationships

Healthy relationships are built on a foundation of mutual respect, trust, communication, and equality. These core principles serve as the bedrock for relationships that enhance the well-being of both partners and allow them to grow individually and together.

Mutual Respect

Respect is the cornerstone of any healthy relationship. It involves recognizing and valuing each other's feelings, thoughts, and boundaries. In a respectful relationship, both partners feel heard and valued. They acknowledge each other's autonomy and do not attempt to control or belittle one another. Respect is demonstrated through active listening, empathy, and a willingness to understand the other person's perspective.

Trust

Trust is essential for a relationship to thrive. It is built over time through consistent, reliable, and honest behavior. Trust involves believing in the other person's integrity and intentions. In a trusting relationship, partners feel safe to express their vulnerabilities without fear of judgment or betrayal. Trust also means keeping promises and being dependable, which reinforces the sense of security within the relationship.

Communication

Effective communication is a vital component of healthy relationships. It involves openly and honestly sharing thoughts, feelings, and needs. Communication should be two-way, with both partners actively listening and responding thoughtfully. Clear and open communication helps prevent misunderstandings, resolve conflicts, and deepen the emotional connection. It also involves expressing oneself assertively, without aggression or passivity, and being willing to engage in difficult conversations constructively.

Equality

Equality in relationships means that both partners have an equal say and power in decision-making. It involves sharing responsibilities and supporting each other's goals and aspirations. In an equal relationship, neither partner dominates or controls the other. Instead, they work together as a team, valuing each other's contributions and ensuring that both partners' needs and desires are considered and respected.

Red Flags to Avoid in Relationships

Recognizing red flags in relationships is crucial for identifying unhealthy dynamics and taking steps to address them. Red flags are warning signs that indicate potential problems or toxic behaviors that can undermine the relationship's health and stability.

Control and Manipulation

One of the most significant red flags is any form of control or manipulation. This can manifest as one partner attempting to dictate the other's actions, choices, or behaviors. Manipulative tactics such as gaslighting, guilt-tripping, and emotional blackmail are harmful and erode trust and respect. In a healthy relationship, both partners should feel free to make their own decisions without coercion.

Lack of Communication

Poor communication or a lack of communication is another red flag. If one or both partners are unwilling or unable to communicate openly and honestly, it can lead to misunderstandings, resentment, and unresolved conflicts. Healthy relationships require ongoing dialogue and a willingness to address issues as they arise.

Disrespect and Criticism

Consistent disrespect or criticism, whether overt or subtle, is a warning sign of an unhealthy relationship. This can include belittling, name-calling, mocking, or dismissing the other person's feelings and opinions. Respect is fundamental to a healthy relationship, and ongoing disrespect can cause significant emotional harm.

Jealousy and Possessiveness

Excessive jealousy or possessiveness can be indicative of insecurity and a lack of trust. While occasional feelings of jealousy are natural, when it becomes a persistent issue or leads to controlling behavior, it undermines the relationship's foundation of trust. Partners should feel confident in their relationship and trust each other without resorting to possessive behaviors.

Imbalance of Power

An imbalance of power, where one partner consistently dominates or controls the other, is a red flag. Healthy relationships are based on equality and shared decision-making. If one partner feels powerless or subordinate, it can lead to feelings of resentment and dissatisfaction.

Isolation

If one partner attempts to isolate the other from friends, family, or support networks, it is a significant warning sign. Isolation can be a tactic used to control and manipulate, making the other person more dependent on the relationship. Healthy relationships encourage and support connections with others outside the partnership.

Strategies for Promoting Mutual Respect and Trust

Promoting mutual respect and trust in a relationship requires intentional effort and commitment from both partners. By implementing strategies that foster these qualities, couples can build a stronger, more resilient bond.

Practice Active Listening

Active listening involves fully engaging with what the other person is saying without interrupting or formulating a response while they are speaking. It requires paying attention, showing empathy, and reflecting on what has been said. Active listening demonstrates respect and validates the other person's feelings and experiences.

Show Appreciation

Regularly expressing appreciation for your partner reinforces positive behaviors and fosters a sense of value and respect. Simple acts of gratitude, such as thanking your partner for their support or acknowledging their efforts, can strengthen the emotional connection and build trust.

Be Honest and Transparent

Honesty is crucial for building trust. Being truthful about your feelings, thoughts, and actions helps create a foundation of reliability and integrity. Transparency involves being open about important aspects of your life, such as finances, past experiences, and future goals. Sharing openly builds trust and reduces the potential for misunderstandings.

Establish Boundaries

Setting and respecting boundaries is essential for maintaining a healthy relationship. Boundaries define what is acceptable and unacceptable behavior and protect each person's autonomy and well-being. Both partners should communicate their boundaries clearly and be willing to respect each other's limits.

Resolve Conflicts Constructively

Conflict is a natural part of any relationship, but how it is managed can significantly impact the relationship's health. Constructive conflict resolution involves addressing issues directly and respectfully, seeking to understand each other's perspectives, and finding mutually acceptable solutions. Avoiding blame, focusing on the problem rather than the person, and being willing to compromise are key aspects of constructive conflict resolution.

Support Each Other's Growth

Encouraging and supporting each other's personal growth and development is a sign of a healthy relationship. This involves respecting each other's goals and aspirations, offering encouragement and support, and celebrating each other's successes. Supporting growth also means being willing to adapt and grow together as a couple.

Spend Quality Time Together

Regularly spending quality time together helps strengthen the emotional bond and fosters a sense of connection and intimacy. Engaging in activities that both partners enjoy, having meaningful conversations, and creating shared experiences can enhance the relationship and build trust.

Seek Help When Needed

Sometimes, external support from a therapist or counselor can be beneficial for addressing relationship challenges and promoting mutual respect and trust. Therapy can provide a safe space for both partners to explore issues, develop better communication skills, and learn strategies for building a healthier relationship.

Establishing healthy relationship dynamics is a continuous process that requires commitment, effort, and mutual respect. By understanding the principles of healthy relationships, recognizing red flags, and implementing strategies for promoting mutual respect and trust, individuals can create and maintain fulfilling and supportive connections. Healthy relationships are characterized by respect, trust, communication, and equality, and they provide a foundation for personal growth and emotional well-being. By actively working to build and maintain these qualities, individuals can foster relationships that are nurturing, empowering, and resilient.

Chapter 10

Legal and Practical Considerations: Seeking Help and Taking Action

In the face of manipulation and abuse, it is crucial for victims to understand the legal protections available to them, the steps to take when dealing with legal issues, and practical advice for seeking help and support. It will provide comprehensive insights into these critical aspects, empowering victims with the knowledge and tools they need to protect themselves and take action.

Legal Protections and Options Available for Victims

Victims of emotional abuse, gaslighting, and psychological manipulation often face numerous challenges, but legal systems in many countries offer protections and options to help them. These protections vary by jurisdiction, but there are several common legal measures designed to safeguard victims and hold abusers accountable.

Restraining Orders and Protection Orders

One of the most common legal protections available is a restraining order, also known as a protection order. These court orders can prohibit the abuser from contacting or coming near the victim, their home, workplace, or other specified locations. Violating a restraining order can result in legal consequences for the abuser, including arrest and prosecution. The process for obtaining a restraining order typically involves filing a petition with the court and providing evidence of abuse or threats. Victims may need to appear in court to testify about their experiences.

Domestic Violence Laws

Many jurisdictions have specific laws addressing domestic violence, which can include emotional and psychological abuse in addition to physical violence. These laws often provide for enhanced penalties for abusers and additional protections for victims. Domestic violence laws may also include provisions for emergency shelters, counseling, and other support services for victims.

Stalking Laws

Stalking is a form of harassment that can include persistent following, monitoring, or unwanted communication. Stalking laws provide legal remedies for victims, such as restraining orders and criminal charges against the stalker. Proving stalking can be challenging, but documenting incidents and maintaining records of communications can be crucial in building a case.

Family Law Protections

In cases where the abuser is a spouse or partner, family law can provide additional protections. This can include provisions for divorce, child custody, and support. Courts can issue temporary orders to protect victims and their children during divorce or custody proceedings, ensuring their safety and well-being.

Workplace Protections

Some jurisdictions have laws protecting victims of domestic violence from discrimination in the workplace. These laws may provide for leave from work to attend court hearings, seek medical treatment, or access counseling services without fear of losing their job. Employers may also be required to provide reasonable accommodations to ensure the safety of victims at work.

Steps to Take When Dealing with Legal Issues

Dealing with legal issues can be daunting, especially for victims of abuse who may already be experiencing fear, confusion, and emotional turmoil. However, taking proactive steps can help navigate the legal system and secure necessary protections.

Document Evidence

Keeping detailed records of incidents of abuse is crucial. This can include dates, times, locations, descriptions of events, and any witnesses. Photographs of injuries, screenshots of threatening messages, and recordings of abusive behavior can also serve as valuable evidence. Documentation can strengthen a case when seeking legal protections or pressing charges.

Seek Legal Advice

Consulting with an attorney who specializes in domestic violence or family law can provide critical guidance. An attorney can explain legal rights, help navigate the legal process, and represent the victim in court. Many organizations offer free or low-cost legal services for victims of abuse, making legal advice more accessible.

File a Police Report

Reporting abuse to law enforcement is an important step in seeking legal protections. A police report can provide an official record of the abuse and initiate a criminal investigation. Victims should provide as much detail as possible and include any evidence they have gathered. It is essential to be honest and thorough when speaking with law enforcement officers.

Obtain a Restraining Order

If there is an immediate threat of harm, victims can petition the court for a restraining order. The process typically involves completing paperwork and providing evidence of the abuse. In some cases, courts may issue temporary restraining orders pending a full hearing. It is important to follow all court instructions and attend all required hearings.

Understand Court Procedures

Navigating the court system can be complex, but understanding court procedures can help. Victims should familiarize themselves with the steps involved in their specific legal process, whether it is obtaining a restraining order, filing for divorce, or pressing criminal charges. Attending court hearings, submitting necessary documents on time, and complying with court orders are all crucial.

Develop a Safety Plan

Legal actions can sometimes escalate an abuser's behavior, making safety planning essential. A safety plan might include staying with friends or family, changing locks, altering routines, and keeping emergency contacts readily available. Local domestic violence organizations can often assist in creating a comprehensive safety plan.

Practical Advice for Seeking Help and Support

In addition to legal protections, practical support is essential for victims of abuse. Various resources and strategies can help victims rebuild their lives and regain their sense of safety and autonomy.

Reach Out to Support Networks

Building a support network is vital for emotional and practical assistance. This can include friends, family, coworkers, and community members who can offer support, listen without judgment, and provide help when needed. Sharing experiences with trusted individuals can reduce feelings of isolation and provide a sense of empowerment.

Utilize Domestic Violence Services

Many communities offer specialized services for victims of domestic violence, including shelters, hotlines, counseling, and legal assistance. Shelters provide a safe place to stay and access to resources such as food, clothing, and medical care. Hotlines can offer immediate support and connect victims with local services. Counseling services can help victims process their experiences and develop coping strategies.

Seek Therapy or Counseling

Therapy can be a powerful tool for healing and recovery. A licensed therapist specializing in trauma or domestic violence can help victims understand their experiences, develop healthy coping mechanisms, and rebuild self-esteem. Support groups can also be beneficial, providing a space to connect with others who have had similar experiences and share strategies for recovery.

Access Financial Resources

Financial dependence on an abuser can be a significant barrier to leaving an abusive relationship. Exploring financial resources and support can help mitigate this challenge. This might include applying for public assistance programs, seeking employment, or accessing emergency funds from local organizations. Some jurisdictions offer financial assistance for victims of domestic violence to help cover expenses such as housing, transportation, and medical care.

Educate Yourself

Knowledge is empowering. Educating oneself about the dynamics of abuse, legal rights, and available resources can provide a sense of control and direction. Many organizations offer educational materials, workshops, and online resources to help victims understand their situation and explore their options.

Prioritize Self-Care

Self-care is essential for recovery and well-being. This can include activities that promote physical health, such as exercise, nutrition, and sleep, as well as practices that support mental and emotional health, such as mindfulness, meditation, and hobbies. Prioritizing self-care helps build resilience and provides a foundation for moving forward.

Create a Personal Support Plan

A personal support plan involves identifying needs and resources, setting goals, and taking steps to achieve them. This plan can include immediate needs, such as finding safe housing, as well as long-term goals, such as pursuing education or career opportunities. Regularly reviewing and updating the plan can help track progress and adapt to changing circumstances.

Engage with Advocacy Organizations

Advocacy organizations play a crucial role in supporting victims of abuse. These organizations work to raise awareness, influence policy, and provide direct services to victims. Engaging with advocacy organizations can offer additional support and opportunities to contribute to broader efforts to combat abuse.

Seeking help and taking action in the face of manipulation and abuse requires courage, determination, and access to the right resources. Understanding legal protections and options, taking proactive steps when dealing with legal issues, and seeking practical support are essential for victims to protect themselves and begin the journey toward healing and empowerment. By building a support network, utilizing available services, and prioritizing self-care, victims can reclaim their lives and establish a future free from abuse.

Chapter 11

Healing from Manipulative Relationships: Recovery and Self-Care

The journey to healing from manipulative relationships is deeply personal, challenging, and transformative. It requires addressing the emotional wounds left by manipulation and abuse, cultivating self-care practices, and building a supportive network that fosters recovery and growth. It looks into strategies for emotional healing, emphasizes the importance of self-care and mental health practices, and underscores the need for a strong support network and professional help.

Strategies for Emotional Healing and Recovery

Emotional healing from manipulative relationships involves recognizing and processing the trauma inflicted by the abuser. It requires patience, self-compassion, and a commitment to reclaiming one's sense of self-worth and identity.

Acknowledging the Pain

The first step in healing is acknowledging the pain and trauma caused by the manipulative relationship. This involves validating one's experiences and emotions, recognizing that the abuse was real and that it had a profound impact. Suppressing or denying the pain only prolongs the healing process. By accepting and facing the emotional wounds, victims can begin to process and work through their trauma.

Understanding the Dynamics of Manipulation

Understanding the tactics and dynamics of manipulation can provide clarity and help victims make sense of their experiences. This knowledge empowers individuals to recognize the patterns of manipulation and avoid falling into similar traps in the future. Education about psychological abuse, gaslighting, and control can also help victims see that the abuse was not their fault and that they were targeted by a manipulator.

Journaling and Expressive Writing

Writing about one's experiences and emotions can be a powerful tool for healing. Journaling provides a safe space to express feelings, reflect on past events, and track progress over time. Expressive writing allows victims to articulate their thoughts and emotions, helping to release pent-up feelings and gain insights into their experiences.

This process can be cathartic and contribute to emotional recovery.

Practicing Self-Compassion

Self-compassion involves treating oneself with the same kindness and understanding that one would offer to a friend. It means acknowledging one's suffering, recognizing that it is part of the human experience, and responding with care rather than self-criticism. Self-compassion can help counteract the negative self-beliefs and low self-esteem often instilled by manipulative relationships.

Reframing Negative Thoughts

Manipulative relationships can leave victims with distorted thinking patterns and negative beliefs about themselves. Cognitive reframing involves challenging these negative thoughts and replacing them with more balanced and positive ones. This process can help shift the internal narrative from one of self-blame and doubt to one of empowerment and self-worth.

Engaging in Creative Activities

Creative activities such as art, music, and dance can provide an outlet for emotional expression and healing. Engaging in creative pursuits allows individuals to process their emotions in non-verbal ways and can bring a sense of joy and fulfillment. Creativity can also serve as a form of self-discovery, helping individuals reconnect with their passions and interests.

Developing New Interests and Goals

Setting new personal goals and pursuing interests that were neglected during the manipulative relationship can be an important part of recovery. This might involve taking up new hobbies, learning new skills, or pursuing educational or career aspirations. Engaging in activities that bring a sense of accomplishment and purpose can boost self-esteem and foster a sense of agency.

Importance of Self-Care and Mental Health Practices

Self-care and mental health practices are crucial for healing from manipulative relationships. They provide the foundation for emotional stability, resilience, and overall well-being.

Establishing Healthy Routines

Creating and maintaining healthy daily routines can provide structure and stability, which are essential for emotional recovery. This includes regular sleep patterns, balanced nutrition, and physical activity. Consistent routines help regulate the body's internal clock and promote a sense of normalcy and control.

Practicing Mindfulness and Meditation

Mindfulness and meditation practices can help individuals stay present and manage stress and anxiety. Mindfulness involves paying attention to the present moment without judgment, while meditation can help calm the mind and reduce emotional reactivity. These practices can enhance self-awareness and provide tools for coping with difficult emotions.

Engaging in Physical Exercise

Physical exercise has numerous benefits for mental health. It can reduce symptoms of depression and anxiety, improve mood, and increase energy levels. Exercise also releases endorphins, which are natural mood lifters. Finding a form of physical activity that is enjoyable, whether it is walking, yoga, dancing, or swimming, can make it easier to incorporate into daily life.

Prioritizing Sleep

Quality sleep is essential for emotional and physical health. Manipulative relationships can often disrupt sleep patterns due to stress and anxiety. Establishing a regular sleep routine, creating a restful sleep environment, and practicing good sleep hygiene can improve sleep quality and contribute to overall well-being.

Seeking Therapeutic Support

Professional therapy can be invaluable in the healing process. Therapists who specialize in trauma and abuse can provide a safe space for victims to explore their experiences, develop coping strategies, and work through emotional pain. Different therapeutic approaches, such as cognitive-behavioral therapy (CBT), eye movement desensitization and reprocessing (EMDR), and trauma-focused therapy, can address various aspects of recovery.

Connecting with Nature

Spending time in nature can have a calming and restorative effect on the mind and body. Activities such as walking in the park, hiking, or simply sitting outdoors can reduce stress, improve mood, and enhance overall mental health. Nature provides a peaceful environment that can promote reflection and healing.

Engaging in Positive Social Activities

Positive social interactions and activities can boost mood and provide a sense of belonging and support. This might involve joining clubs, participating in group activities, or attending social events. Engaging with others in a positive and supportive context can help counteract feelings of isolation and loneliness.

Building a Support Network and Seeking Professional Help

A strong support network and access to professional help are essential components of healing from manipulative relationships. They provide emotional support, practical assistance, and validation, helping victims feel less alone and more empowered.

Identifying Supportive Individuals

Building a support network starts with identifying individuals who are trustworthy, empathetic, and supportive. This might include friends, family members, coworkers, or members of community groups. It is important to reach out to those who offer genuine support and understanding, and who respect boundaries and confidentiality.

Joining Support Groups

Support groups for survivors of abuse provide a safe space to share experiences, receive validation, and connect with others who have been through similar situations. These groups can offer a sense of community and understanding that is often difficult to find elsewhere. Support groups can also provide practical advice and resources for navigating the healing process.

Accessing Community Resources

Many communities offer resources for victims of abuse, such as crisis hotlines, shelters, counseling services, and legal assistance. These resources can provide immediate support and assistance in times of need. Victims should not hesitate to seek out these services, as they are designed to help individuals in their recovery journey.

Seeking Professional Therapy

Professional therapy is a crucial component of healing for many victims. Therapists can help individuals process their trauma, develop coping strategies, and rebuild their self-esteem. Different therapeutic approaches can address various aspects of recovery, and it may be necessary to try different methods to find the one that works best.

Engaging in Peer Support

Peer support involves connecting with others who have experienced similar challenges and can offer empathy, understanding, and practical advice. This can include one-on-one peer support or participation in online forums and discussion groups. Peer support can provide a sense of solidarity and reduce feelings of isolation.

Establishing Boundaries

Establishing and maintaining boundaries is essential for emotional well-being. This includes setting limits with others, protecting personal space and time, and ensuring that relationships are respectful and supportive. Boundaries help create a sense of safety and autonomy, which is crucial for recovery.

Developing a Safety Plan

For those who are still in contact with their abuser or fear further manipulation, developing a safety plan is important. This might include identifying safe places to go, having emergency contacts readily available, and creating a plan for safely exiting dangerous situations. A safety plan can provide a sense of security and preparedness.

Educating Loved Ones

Educating friends and family about the dynamics of manipulative relationships and the healing process can foster understanding and support. Loved ones who are informed about the challenges and needs of the victim can offer more effective and empathetic support. Providing educational materials and resources can help them understand the complexities of recovery.

Healing from manipulative relationships is a multifaceted process that involves emotional healing, self-care, and building a supportive network. By employing strategies for emotional recovery, prioritizing self-care and mental health practices, and seeking support from trusted individuals and professionals, victims can reclaim their lives and move towards a future of empowerment and well-being. The journey to healing is not linear, and it requires patience, resilience, and self-compassion. However, with the right tools and support, it is possible to heal, grow, and thrive beyond the shadows of manipulation and abuse.

Chapter 12

Educational Approaches: Learning About Manipulation and Abuse

Understanding and addressing manipulation and abuse requires comprehensive educational approaches. Workshops, courses, and educational resources are essential for equipping individuals with the knowledge and skills to recognize and respond to manipulation. Training programs, guest speakers, and experts in psychology and relationship dynamics play crucial roles in fostering awareness and providing practical tools for both prevention and intervention.

Workshops, Courses, and Educational Resources on Manipulation

Education is a powerful tool in the fight against manipulation and abuse. Workshops and courses designed to address these issues provide structured learning experiences that can make a significant impact on individuals and communities.

Workshops on Emotional and Psychological Abuse: Workshops focused on emotional and psychological abuse offer a safe space for participants to learn about the various forms of manipulation, including gaslighting, control tactics, and emotional coercion. These workshops often include interactive activities, discussions, and case studies that help participants understand the subtle and overt signs of manipulation. By engaging in these activities, participants can better identify abusive behaviors and learn effective strategies for responding to them.

Courses on Healthy Relationships

Educational courses on healthy relationships are essential for fostering awareness and prevention. These courses cover topics such as communication skills, conflict resolution, and boundary-setting. By teaching individuals what constitutes a healthy relationship, these courses help them recognize unhealthy dynamics and understand the importance of mutual respect and equality in relationships. Participants learn to identify red flags and develop skills to maintain healthy interactions.

Online Educational Resources

The internet offers a wealth of educational resources on manipulation and abuse. Online courses, webinars, and e-books provide accessible and flexible learning options for individuals seeking to educate themselves on these issues.

Websites dedicated to abuse prevention and support often offer comprehensive guides, fact sheets, and self-assessment tools that help individuals understand their experiences and find appropriate resources. Online forums and support groups also provide a platform for sharing experiences and gaining insights from others who have faced similar challenges.

Interactive E-Learning Modules

E-learning modules are designed to engage learners through interactive content, including videos, quizzes, and simulations. These modules can be particularly effective in teaching individuals how to recognize manipulation and respond appropriately. By simulating real-life scenarios, e-learning modules provide practical experience in a controlled environment, allowing participants to practice their responses and build confidence in their ability to handle manipulative situations.

Training Programs for Recognizing and Responding to Manipulation

Training programs are vital for empowering individuals to recognize and respond to manipulation effectively. These programs can be tailored for various audiences, including professionals, community leaders, and the general public.

Professional Training for Therapists and Counselors

Therapists and counselors play a critical role in supporting victims of manipulation and abuse. Specialized training programs for these professionals focus on the dynamics of abuse, the psychological impact on victims, and effective therapeutic interventions. Training covers assessment techniques, trauma-informed care, and strategies for helping clients rebuild their self-esteem and resilience. By equipping therapists and counselors with the necessary knowledge and skills, these programs ensure that victims receive informed and compassionate support.

Training for Educators and School Staff

Schools are important settings for early intervention and prevention. Training programs for educators and school staff aim to create a safe and supportive environment for students. These programs educate school personnel on the signs of manipulation and abuse, including bullying and cyberbullying. They also provide strategies for addressing these issues, supporting affected students, and promoting a culture of respect and inclusion. By fostering awareness among educators, these programs help protect students from manipulative behaviors and create a foundation for healthy relationships.

Corporate Training Programs

Workplaces can also be environments where manipulation and abuse occur. Corporate training programs focus on creating a respectful and safe workplace culture. These programs educate employees and managers on recognizing and addressing manipulative behaviors, such as harassment, bullying, and power imbalances. Training includes communication skills, conflict resolution techniques, and policies for reporting and addressing abuse. By promoting a positive and respectful workplace, these programs help prevent manipulation and support employees who may be experiencing abuse.

Community-Based Training Initiatives

Community organizations play a vital role in supporting victims and raising awareness about manipulation and abuse. Community-based training initiatives involve workshops, seminars, and public awareness campaigns designed to educate community members on these issues. Training covers the signs of abuse, available resources, and ways to support victims. By engaging community members, these initiatives create a network of informed and proactive individuals who can contribute to prevention and support efforts.

Law Enforcement Training

Law enforcement officers are often the first responders to situations involving manipulation and abuse. Training programs for law enforcement focus on recognizing the signs of emotional and psychological abuse, understanding the dynamics of manipulation, and responding with sensitivity and professionalism. Training includes techniques for interviewing victims, collecting evidence, and providing referrals to support services. By equipping law enforcement with the knowledge and skills to handle these cases effectively, these programs enhance the protection and support available to victims.

Guest Speakers and Experts in the Field of Psychology and Relationship Dynamics

Guest speakers and experts in psychology and relationship dynamics bring valuable insights and expertise to educational efforts. Their contributions can enhance understanding, provide inspiration, and offer practical guidance.

Psychologists and Therapists

Psychologists and therapists with expertise in trauma, manipulation, and abuse provide in-depth knowledge on the psychological impact of these experiences. They can offer insights into the emotional and cognitive processes involved in manipulation, helping participants understand how abusers exploit vulnerabilities. These experts can also share therapeutic approaches and techniques for supporting victims in their healing journey. Their presentations often include case studies, research findings, and practical advice for both victims and those supporting them.

Survivors and Advocates

Hearing from survivors of manipulation and abuse can be profoundly impactful. Survivor speakers share their personal stories, highlighting the realities of abuse and the challenges of recovery. Their experiences provide validation and hope for others who are going through similar situations. Survivor speakers often become advocates, working to raise awareness and promote change. Their presentations can inspire action and underscore the importance of support and intervention.

Legal Experts

Legal experts provide crucial information on the legal protections available to victims of manipulation and abuse. They can explain the process for obtaining restraining orders, pressing charges, and navigating the legal system. Legal experts also discuss the rights of victims and the responsibilities of law enforcement and judicial systems. By educating participants on legal options and procedures, these experts empower victims to take action and seek justice.

Relationship and Communication Specialists

Specialists in relationship dynamics and communication provide practical tools for building healthy relationships and addressing manipulation. They teach skills such as assertiveness, boundary-setting, and conflict resolution. These experts also discuss the importance of mutual respect, trust, and effective communication in relationships. Their presentations offer actionable strategies for improving relationship dynamics and preventing manipulation.

Researchers and Academics

Researchers and academics contribute valuable insights from their studies on manipulation, abuse, and trauma. They share research findings, theories, and evidence-based practices that inform prevention and intervention efforts. Academic presentations can provide a broader context for understanding manipulation and abuse, highlighting patterns, risk factors, and effective interventions. By bridging the gap between research and practice, these experts enhance the effectiveness of educational efforts.

Educational approaches to learning about manipulation and abuse are essential for prevention, intervention, and support. Workshops, courses, and educational resources provide structured learning experiences that empower individuals with knowledge and skills. Training programs equip professionals, educators, and community members to recognize and respond to manipulation effectively. Guest speakers and experts in psychology and relationship dynamics offer valuable insights, inspiration, and practical guidance. By fostering awareness and providing practical tools, these educational approaches contribute to a safer, more informed, and supportive society, enabling individuals to recognize, address, and recover from manipulation and abuse.

Chapter 13

Social and Community Support: Finding Networks of Understanding

Healing from manipulation and abuse is a journey that often requires more than personal resilience; it demands a network of understanding and support. Social and community support systems, including online forums, local resources, and peer counseling, play a crucial role in this recovery process. These networks provide victims with validation, guidance, and companionship, helping them to navigate the complexities of healing. It explores the various avenues of social and community support, highlighting their significance and effectiveness in aiding survivors.

Online Forums and Support Groups for Victims of Manipulation

In an increasingly digital world, online forums and support groups have become vital resources for victims of manipulation and abuse. These platforms offer anonymity, accessibility, and a sense of community, making them invaluable for those seeking understanding and support.

Anonymity and Safety

One of the primary advantages of online forums is the anonymity they provide. Victims can share their experiences and seek advice without revealing their identities, which can be particularly important for those who fear retaliation or judgment. This anonymity allows for candid discussions and enables victims to express their emotions and concerns freely, fostering a sense of safety and trust within the community.

24/7 Accessibility

Online support groups are accessible at any time, providing immediate assistance to those in need. This round-the-clock availability is crucial, as crises and emotional distress can occur at any hour. Participants can post their thoughts and receive responses from others who understand their experiences, offering timely comfort and advice.

Global Community

The internet connects people from all over the world, creating a diverse and inclusive support network. Victims can interact with individuals from different backgrounds, cultures, and experiences, broadening their perspectives and finding solidarity in shared experiences. This global community reinforces the notion that they are not alone in their struggles and that manipulation and abuse are widespread issues.

Educational Resources

Many online forums and support groups provide educational resources on manipulation and abuse. These resources include articles, videos, and guides that help victims understand the dynamics of abuse, recognize red flags, and learn coping strategies. Access to this information empowers victims to make informed decisions and take proactive steps toward healing.

Moderation and Professional Input

Reputable online support groups often have moderators and professionals who ensure the discussions remain supportive and respectful. Moderators can intervene in conflicts, provide additional resources, and offer professional insights. This structured environment enhances the quality of support and ensures that victims receive accurate and helpful information.

Local Community Resources for Survivors of Abuse

Local community resources offer essential support to survivors of abuse, providing practical assistance, emotional support, and a sense of belonging. These resources are often tailored to the specific needs of the community, ensuring that survivors have access to relevant and effective help.

Shelters and Safe Houses

Shelters and safe houses provide immediate refuge for those escaping abusive situations. These facilities offer a secure environment where survivors can stay temporarily while they work on rebuilding their lives. In addition to providing basic necessities such as food and shelter, these facilities often offer counseling, legal assistance, and job placement services to help survivors transition to independent living.

Counseling and Support Services

Local community centers frequently offer counseling and support services for survivors of abuse. These services may include individual therapy, group therapy, and crisis counseling. Trained professionals help survivors process their trauma, develop coping strategies, and work toward emotional recovery. Community centers also provide referrals to specialized services, ensuring that survivors receive comprehensive care.

Legal Assistance

Navigating the legal system can be daunting for survivors of abuse. Local resources often include legal assistance programs that help survivors understand their rights, file restraining orders, and pursue legal action against their abusers. Legal advocates can accompany survivors to court, provide guidance on legal procedures, and ensure that their voices are heard in legal matters.

Support Groups

In-person support groups offer a space for survivors to share their experiences, receive validation, and connect with others who have faced similar challenges. These groups are typically led by trained facilitators who guide discussions and provide a safe and supportive environment. Support groups foster a sense of community and help survivors build relationships with others who understand their struggles.

Educational Workshops and Seminars

Many local organizations host workshops and seminars on topics related to abuse and recovery. These educational events cover a range of subjects, including recognizing signs of abuse, building healthy relationships, and developing self-care practices. Workshops and seminars provide valuable information and practical skills that empower survivors to take control of their lives and make informed decisions.

Hotlines and Crisis Intervention

Crisis hotlines provide immediate support to survivors in distress. These hotlines are staffed by trained professionals who offer emotional support, safety planning, and referrals to local resources. Crisis intervention services can also include mobile crisis teams that respond to emergency situations and provide on-site support and assessment.

Peer Counseling and Group Therapy Options for Healing and Recovery

Peer counseling and group therapy are powerful tools for healing and recovery, offering survivors a platform to share their experiences, gain insights, and develop coping strategies in a supportive environment.

Peer Counseling

Peer counseling involves individuals who have experienced similar challenges providing support and guidance to each other. Peer counselors are often survivors of abuse themselves, making them uniquely qualified to understand and empathize with the struggles of others. This form of support fosters a sense of camaraderie and mutual understanding, helping survivors feel less isolated and more connected.

Training for Peer Counselors

Effective peer counseling programs include training for peer counselors to ensure they provide appropriate and helpful support. Training covers active listening, empathy, confidentiality, and crisis intervention techniques. Peer counselors learn how to create a safe and supportive environment, recognize signs of distress, and provide referrals to professional services when necessary.

Benefits of Peer Counseling

Peer counseling offers several benefits, including relatability, validation, and empowerment. Survivors often find it easier to open up to someone who has been through similar experiences, leading to more honest and meaningful conversations. Peer counseling also provides a sense of empowerment, as survivors can see that others have successfully navigated similar challenges and achieved recovery.

Group Therapy

Group therapy involves a therapist or counselor leading a group of individuals who share similar experiences. This structured environment provides a safe space for participants to discuss their feelings, share coping strategies, and receive feedback from both the therapist and other group members. Group therapy can address a range of issues, including trauma, anxiety, and depression, all of which are common among survivors of abuse.

Healing Through Shared Experiences

Group therapy allows participants to hear different perspectives and learn from the experiences of others. This shared understanding fosters a sense of community and helps participants realize they are not alone in their struggles. Group members can offer support, encouragement, and practical advice, creating a network of care and understanding.

Building Trust and Connection

Trust is a crucial component of healing, and group therapy provides a space where survivors can build trust with others. By sharing their stories and supporting each other, group members develop strong connections that contribute to their emotional recovery. These relationships can extend beyond the therapy sessions, providing ongoing support and friendship.

Tailored Group Therapy Programs

Group therapy programs can be tailored to address specific needs and issues. For example, some groups may focus on trauma recovery, while others may address relationship dynamics or self-esteem. Tailored programs ensure that participants receive relevant and focused support that addresses their unique experiences and challenges.

Combining Group Therapy with Individual Therapy

Many survivors find that combining group therapy with individual therapy offers a comprehensive approach to healing. Individual therapy provides personalized support and focuses on specific issues, while group therapy offers the benefits of shared experiences and community support. Together, these therapeutic approaches can enhance the overall effectiveness of the healing process.

Social and community support systems are vital for the recovery and healing of survivors of manipulation and abuse. Online forums and support groups provide anonymity, accessibility, and a global community of understanding. Local community resources offer practical assistance, counseling, legal support, and educational opportunities. Peer counseling and group therapy create environments where survivors can share their experiences, gain insights, and build connections with others who understand their struggles. By leveraging these support systems, survivors can find the validation, guidance, and companionship they need to navigate the complexities of healing and reclaim their lives. The journey to recovery is strengthened by the networks of understanding and support that surround and uplift survivors, helping them to overcome the challenges they face and move toward a brighter, more empowered future.

Chapter 14

Advocacy and Awareness: Spreading Knowledge and Empathy

Understanding and addressing the pervasive issue of manipulation and abuse requires concerted efforts in advocacy and awareness. These endeavors aim to educate the public, influence legislation, and foster empathy in personal and professional relationships. Campaigns and initiatives play a crucial role in raising awareness, while advocacy efforts work to enact and support policies that protect victims. Promoting empathy and understanding is essential for creating a culture where manipulation and abuse are not tolerated. It looks into the multifaceted approaches necessary to spread knowledge and cultivate a compassionate society.

Campaigns and Initiatives to Raise Awareness About Manipulation and Abuse

Awareness campaigns are pivotal in educating the public about the often hidden and insidious nature of manipulation and abuse. These initiatives aim to inform, engage, and mobilize individuals and communities to recognize, prevent, and address abusive behaviors.

Public Awareness Campaigns

Public awareness campaigns are designed to reach a broad audience through various media channels, including television, radio, social media, and print media. These campaigns often feature powerful messages, survivor stories, and educational content that highlight the signs of manipulation and abuse. By increasing visibility and understanding, these campaigns help break the stigma and silence surrounding these issues.

Social Media Initiatives

Social media platforms are potent tools for spreading awareness and engaging a global audience. Hashtag campaigns, informational posts, and survivor testimonies shared on platforms like Twitter, Facebook, and Instagram can reach millions, fostering a collective awareness. Social media initiatives also allow for interactive engagement, where individuals can share their experiences, offer support, and participate in online discussions.

Educational Workshops and Seminars

Hosting educational workshops and seminars in schools, workplaces, and community centers is another effective way to raise awareness. These events provide in-depth information on the dynamics of manipulation and abuse, teaching participants how to recognize red flags and respond appropriately. Workshops and seminars also offer a space for open dialogue, enabling attendees to ask questions and share their experiences.

Survivor-Led Initiatives

Survivors of manipulation and abuse often lead powerful initiatives that bring a personal and impactful perspective to awareness efforts. By sharing their stories, survivors can inspire and educate others, highlighting the realities of abuse and the importance of support and intervention. Survivor-led initiatives can include speaking engagements, written testimonials, and participation in awareness campaigns.

Collaborations with Influencers and Celebrities

Collaborating with influencers and celebrities can amplify the reach and impact of awareness campaigns. Public figures who speak out against manipulation and abuse can draw significant attention to the cause, encouraging their followers to become informed and involved. These collaborations can include public service announcements, social media posts, and participation in awareness events.

Community Art Projects

Community art projects, such as murals, exhibitions, and performance art, can convey powerful messages about manipulation and abuse. These projects engage the community in creative expression, raising awareness through visual and experiential mediums. Art projects can also serve as a therapeutic outlet for survivors, allowing them to share their experiences and contribute to the awareness effort.

Advocacy Efforts to Support Legislation and Policies Protecting Victims

Advocacy efforts are essential for driving systemic change and ensuring that victims of manipulation and abuse are protected by robust legislation and policies. These efforts involve lobbying for legal reforms, supporting existing protections, and promoting policies that prioritize victim safety and support.

Lobbying for Legal Reforms

Advocacy groups work tirelessly to lobby for legal reforms that enhance protections for victims of manipulation and abuse. This includes advocating for stricter penalties for perpetrators, expanding definitions of abuse to include emotional and psychological manipulation, and ensuring that laws address all forms of abuse. Lobbying efforts often involve working with lawmakers, providing testimony, and mobilizing public support to influence legislative change.

Supporting Existing Protections

Advocacy efforts also focus on supporting and enforcing existing legal protections for victims. This includes ensuring that restraining orders and other protective measures are accessible and effectively implemented. Advocacy groups may provide resources and support to help victims navigate the legal system, ensuring they receive the protection they need.

Promoting Policies for Victim Support

Policies that prioritize victim support are crucial for helping survivors rebuild their lives. Advocacy efforts work to promote policies that provide comprehensive services, including counseling, housing, legal assistance, and financial support. These policies should aim to address the multifaceted needs of survivors, ensuring they have the resources necessary to recover and thrive.

Engaging in Grassroots Advocacy

Grassroots advocacy involves mobilizing community members to take action on behalf of victims of manipulation and abuse. This can include organizing petitions, hosting rallies, and engaging in public education efforts. Grassroots movements harness the power of collective action, bringing attention to critical issues and driving change from the ground up.

Coalition Building

Building coalitions with other advocacy groups, non-profit organizations, and community stakeholders strengthens the impact of advocacy efforts. Coalitions can work together to share resources, coordinate actions, and amplify their voices. By uniting for a common cause, these groups can exert greater influence on policy decisions and public opinion.

Media Advocacy

Utilizing media to advocate for policy change is an effective strategy for raising awareness and influencing decision-makers. Advocacy groups can engage with journalists, write op-eds, and use social media to highlight the need for stronger protections and support for victims. Media advocacy helps bring these issues to the forefront of public discourse, increasing pressure on lawmakers to act.

Promoting Empathy and Understanding in Personal and Professional Relationships

Fostering empathy and understanding is essential for preventing manipulation and abuse and promoting healthy, respectful relationships. By cultivating these qualities in personal and professional interactions, individuals and communities can create environments where abuse is less likely to occur and more easily addressed.

Education on Empathy

Teaching empathy involves educating individuals about the importance of understanding and sharing the feelings of others. This can be done through workshops, training programs, and educational materials that focus on emotional intelligence, active listening, and compassionate communication. By learning to empathize, individuals can better recognize the impact of their actions on others and develop more supportive relationships.

Modeling Empathetic Behavior

Leaders and influencers in personal and professional settings can model empathetic behavior, setting a standard for others to follow. This includes demonstrating respect, actively listening, and responding with compassion and understanding. By modeling these behaviors, leaders can create a culture of empathy that permeates the entire community or organization.

Encouraging Open Communication

Open communication is vital for fostering empathy and understanding. Creating spaces where individuals feel safe to express their thoughts and emotions without fear of judgment or retaliation encourages honest and meaningful interactions. This openness helps build trust and ensures that concerns and issues are addressed constructively.

Conflict Resolution Training

Training in conflict resolution equips individuals with the skills to manage disagreements and conflicts in a healthy and respectful manner. This training can include techniques for active listening, problem-solving, and finding mutually beneficial solutions. By handling conflicts with empathy and understanding, individuals can prevent escalation and maintain positive relationships.

Workplace Policies and Training

Implementing workplace policies that promote respect and empathy is essential for preventing manipulation and abuse in professional settings. This can include anti-harassment policies, diversity and inclusion training, and programs that encourage teamwork and collaboration. Training employees on these policies and practices ensures that the workplace remains a safe and supportive environment.

Empathy in Leadership

Leaders who prioritize empathy create a supportive and inclusive environment. Empathetic leaders listen to their team members, value their input, and respond to their needs. This leadership style fosters loyalty, engagement, and a sense of belonging, reducing the likelihood of manipulation and abuse.

Supportive Community Networks

Building supportive community networks involves creating groups and spaces where individuals can connect, share experiences, and support one another. These networks can include support groups, mentorship programs, and community events that encourage positive interactions and mutual respect. By fostering a sense of community and belonging, these networks help individuals feel valued and understood.

Advocacy and awareness efforts are crucial for addressing manipulation and abuse, protecting victims, and fostering empathy and understanding. Campaigns and initiatives play a vital role in raising public awareness, educating individuals, and breaking the silence surrounding abuse. Advocacy efforts drive legal and policy changes that ensure victims receive the protection and support they need. Promoting empathy and understanding in personal and professional relationships creates environments where manipulation and abuse are less likely to occur and more easily addressed. Through these combined efforts, we can build a society that recognizes, prevents, and responds to manipulation and abuse, supporting survivors on their journey to healing and creating a culture of respect and compassion.

Chapter 15

Continuing Education: Developing Skills for Long-Term Resilience

Continuing education plays a pivotal role in cultivating long-term resilience by equipping individuals with the knowledge and skills needed to navigate psychological challenges and maintain healthy relationships. It explores ongoing learning opportunities in psychology and emotional intelligence, professional development courses for improving communication skills, and strategies for sustaining boundaries and nurturing healthy relationships over time.

Ongoing Learning Opportunities in Psychology and Emotional Intelligence

Continuing education in psychology and emotional intelligence provides individuals with insights into human behavior, emotional regulation, and interpersonal dynamics. These opportunities help individuals deepen their understanding of themselves and others, fostering resilience and adaptive coping mechanisms in the face of adversity.

Psychology Workshops and Seminars

Workshops and seminars on psychology cover a range of topics, including cognitive-behavioral therapy (CBT), trauma-informed care, and resilience-building techniques. These educational sessions are led by experts in the field who share evidence-based practices and practical strategies for managing stress, improving self-awareness, and enhancing emotional well-being.

Online Courses in Emotional Intelligence

Online courses offer flexible learning options for individuals interested in enhancing their emotional intelligence. These courses explore key competencies such as self-awareness, self-regulation, empathy, and social skills. Participants learn practical techniques for recognizing and managing emotions, improving communication, and building stronger relationships both personally and professionally.

Continuing Education Programs

Many universities and professional organizations offer continuing education programs in psychology and emotional intelligence. These programs may include certificate courses, workshops, and conferences that provide in-depth knowledge and skills relevant to mental health, counseling, and interpersonal effectiveness.

Participants gain valuable insights into human behavior and psychological principles that can be applied in various personal and professional settings.

Reading and Self-Study

Continuous learning can also be pursued through reading books, research articles, and online resources on psychology and emotional intelligence. Self-study allows individuals to explore specific topics of interest at their own pace, deepening their knowledge and understanding of psychological concepts and practical applications for resilience.

Peer Learning and Discussion Groups

Engaging in peer learning and discussion groups provides opportunities for individuals to exchange ideas, share experiences, and learn from each other's perspectives. These informal settings promote collaborative learning and mutual support, allowing participants to gain new insights and strategies for enhancing resilience and emotional intelligence.

Professional Development Courses for Improving Communication Skills

Effective communication is essential for maintaining healthy relationships and navigating interpersonal dynamics. Professional development courses focus on enhancing communication skills, promoting clarity, empathy, and mutual understanding in both personal and professional interactions.

Communication Workshops

Workshops on communication skills cover essential topics such as active listening, assertiveness, conflict resolution, and nonverbal communication. Participants learn practical techniques for expressing themselves clearly, understanding others' perspectives, and fostering constructive dialogue in various contexts.

Public Speaking and Presentation Skills

Courses in public speaking and presentation skills equip individuals with the confidence and ability to communicate effectively in front of audiences. These skills are valuable for conveying ideas persuasively, engaging listeners, and building rapport through compelling storytelling and effective delivery.

Negotiation and Mediation Training

Training in negotiation and mediation enhances individuals' ability to resolve conflicts and negotiate mutually beneficial agreements. Participants learn strategies for managing disagreements, finding common ground, and achieving positive outcomes through collaborative problem-solving and effective communication techniques.

Cross-Cultural Communication

In today's globalized world, cross-cultural communication skills are essential for navigating cultural differences and building inclusive relationships. Courses in cross-cultural communication teach individuals to recognize cultural norms, adapt communication styles, and promote cultural sensitivity in diverse environments.

Feedback and Coaching Skills

Developing skills in providing constructive feedback and coaching enables individuals to support others' professional growth and development. These courses focus on delivering feedback effectively, fostering a growth mindset, and guiding individuals toward achieving their goals through supportive and empowering interactions.

Strategies for Maintaining Boundaries and Healthy Relationships Over Time

Maintaining boundaries and nurturing healthy relationships are foundational for long-term resilience and well-being. Strategies focus on self-awareness, assertiveness, and self-care practices that support individuals in preserving their emotional and psychological boundaries while fostering positive connections with others.

Self-Awareness Practices

Cultivating self-awareness involves reflecting on personal values, emotions, and boundaries. Through mindfulness, journaling, and self-reflection exercises, individuals gain clarity about their needs, preferences, and limits, enabling them to communicate effectively and assertively in relationships.

Setting Clear Boundaries

Establishing clear boundaries involves communicating expectations and limits to others in a respectful manner. Individuals learn to identify their boundaries regarding time, space, emotions, and behaviors, creating a framework for healthy interactions and mutual respect in personal and professional relationships.

Assertiveness Training

Assertiveness training teaches individuals to express their thoughts, feelings, and needs confidently and respectfully. Techniques such as "I" statements, assertive body language, and active listening empower individuals to advocate for themselves while considering others' perspectives and maintaining positive relationships.

Conflict Resolution Skills

Developing skills in conflict resolution enables individuals to address disagreements constructively and maintain harmony in relationships. Strategies include active listening, empathy, problem-solving, and negotiation techniques that promote mutual understanding, compromise, and effective communication.

Self-Care Practices

Prioritizing self-care is essential for maintaining emotional resilience and preventing burnout in personal and professional relationships. Self-care practices may include physical exercise, relaxation techniques, hobbies, and activities that promote relaxation, rejuvenation, and overall well-being.

Boundary Maintenance Strategies

Consistently enforcing boundaries involves recognizing and responding to boundary violations assertively and effectively. Individuals learn to set consequences for boundary breaches, seek support from trusted individuals or professionals, and prioritize their own well-being in challenging situations.

Continuing education plays a vital role in developing skills for long-term resilience, enhancing psychological understanding, improving communication, and maintaining healthy relationships over time. Ongoing learning opportunities in psychology and emotional intelligence provide insights into human behavior and emotional regulation, fostering adaptive coping mechanisms and resilience. Professional development courses focus on communication skills, promoting clarity, empathy, and effective dialogue in personal and professional interactions. Strategies for maintaining boundaries and nurturing healthy relationships involve self-awareness, assertiveness, conflict resolution, and self-care practices that support individuals in preserving their emotional well-being and fostering positive connections with others. By investing in continuous learning and skill development, individuals can strengthen their resilience and thrive in diverse personal and professional environments, contributing to their overall happiness and success.

Conclusion

As we conclude this journey through the complexities of dealing with manipulative relationships, it's essential to reflect on the key learnings and insights gained from our exploration. Throughout this book, we have uncovered the insidious tactics of manipulation and abuse, examined the emotional and psychological impacts on victims, and explored strategies for recognizing, addressing, and overcoming these challenges.

We've learned that manipulation often operates subtly, undermining our sense of self-worth and autonomy. It can manifest in various forms, from gaslighting and emotional abuse to coercive control and exploitation. Understanding these tactics is crucial for recognizing when we are being manipulated and for taking decisive action to protect ourselves.

Empowerment begins with awareness—an awareness of our own boundaries, values, and rights. By cultivating self-awareness and emotional intelligence, we equip ourselves with the tools to assert our boundaries confidently and to navigate relationships with clarity and resilience. We've explored the importance of seeking support from trusted individuals, communities, and professionals who can provide validation, guidance, and practical assistance on our journey to healing.

Now, armed with knowledge and insights, it's time to take action. Empowerment is not merely a concept; it is a journey of reclaiming our power and agency. It starts with setting boundaries and enforcing them, recognizing our worth, and refusing to tolerate manipulation or abuse in any form. It involves prioritizing our mental and emotional well-being, practicing self-care, and seeking professional help when needed.

Taking steps towards empowerment means embracing our strengths and vulnerabilities alike, learning from our experiences, and committing to personal growth and resilience. It's about fostering healthy self-esteem and cultivating relationships based on mutual respect, trust, and reciprocity.

Ultimately, creating a life filled with healthy, respectful relationships requires intentional effort and continuous commitment. It involves communicating openly and honestly, listening actively, and empathizing with others' perspectives. It means honoring our own needs and boundaries while respecting those of others, fostering empathy, and understanding in all interactions.

Healthy relationships are built on a foundation of trust, communication, and mutual support. They thrive on authenticity, compassion, and shared values. By nurturing these qualities within ourselves and our relationships, we create spaces where manipulation and abuse have no place, where authenticity and respect reign supreme.

Remember that your journey towards healing and empowerment is unique and ongoing. It's a journey that requires courage, self-reflection, and resilience. Embrace the lessons learned, celebrate your strengths, and continue to grow into the empowered individual you are meant to be. Together, let's strive to cultivate a world where healthy, respectful relationships flourish, and where each person can live authentically and thrive.